Guidelines for Developing
a Criminal Justice
Coordinating Committee

Robert C. Cushman

January 2002

NIC Accession Number 017232

This guide was prepared under technical assistance event No. 99J1125 from the National Institute of Corrections, U.S. Department of Justice. Points of view or opinions stated in this guide are those of the author and do not necessarily represent the official position or policies of the U.S. Department of Justice.

Foreword

This document provides guidelines for establishing a local criminal justice coordinating committee (CJCC). It describes CJCCs and provides specific guidance for their development and operation.

The guide will help appointed and elected officials of general government and executives of local justice systems from jurisdictions of all sizes create or strengthen local CJCCs. It should be of particular interest to citizens and public officials who sense that more collaborative, better coordinated decisionmaking processes can improve the local criminal justice system significantly.

During a strategic planning process of the National Institute of Corrections (NIC) Jails Division, staff noted that many of the consultants conducting site visits to local jurisdictions were recommending that those jurisdictions strengthen their local planning, analysis, and coordinating capabilities. In many cases, the consultants were recommending the formation of a broad-based

CJCC. This was particularly true of NIC-sponsored technical assistance designed to help communities cope with jail crowding. NIC has found, in many cases, that what a community was treating as solely a "jail problem" was, instead, a systemwide condition requiring an intergovernmental and interagency response.

We hope this guide will assist others who wish to improve communication, cooperation, and coordination in their local criminal justice system. We invite all criminal justice practitioners involved in this work to contact the NIC Jails Division for additional assistance if needed. Contact information for the Jails Division and other CJCC resources is provided in appendix C of this guide.

Morris L. Thigpen
Director
National Institute of Corrections

Preface and Acknowledgments

This guide was developed to assist the communities being served by NIC technical assistance programs and the NIC consultants providing technical assistance. It lays the groundwork for understanding the relationship between a CJCC's operations and its impact on jail crowding and for many other system improvements.

Many people and organizations contributed ideas and materials to this guide. It is impossible to thank them all individually. The CJCCs mentioned in this guide are listed in an appendix; each contributed in some way. In addition, many other colleagues, staff members, and CJCC members have contributed ideas found in these pages.

Richard Geaither, a correctional program specialist at the NIC Jails Division, has served as an initiator, supporter, and adviser of this work; he also has served as NIC monitor.

I want to thank Patricia Carrillo for production support. Also, I am indebted to Katie Ryan for her editorial assistance and to Karen Swetlow of Aspen Systems Corporation, who edited the final version of this guide and coordinated its production.

Robert C. Cushman
November 2001

Contents

List of Exhibits

Executive Summary

This guide will be useful to anyone who wishes to establish or strengthen a criminal justice coordinating committee (CJCC) or learn how a CJCC can alleviate jail crowding and accomplish other system improvements. "Criminal justice coordinating committee" is an inclusive term applied to informal and formal committees that provide a forum where many key justice system agency officials and other officials of general government may discuss justice system issues.

This guide offers advice on how CJCCs can be initiated within local governments, describes the range of planning and coordinating activities that might be undertaken, describes alternative organizational forms for CJCCs, presents guidelines for operating a CJCC, and describes the benefits local governments can expect to derive from these activities.

CJCCs: The Need

Administration of the justice system is primarily a responsibility of local governments. In many cities and counties, a sentiment is expressed that the system of criminal justice should, and could, work better. Scarce local resources could be allocated more efficiently if city and county law enforcement activities, court practices, and corrections programs were planned and conducted in a coordinated fashion.

This sentiment is especially acute in jurisdictions where jail crowding is a severe or chronic problem. This guide provides an answer to those who ask: Could improved planning and coordination reverse crowding in correctional institutions and work overload in other justice agencies? Could a systemwide, interagency, and intergovernmental CJCC help in this area?

CJCCs: The Advantages

The work of CJCCs can produce many benefits, including better understanding of crime and criminal justice problems, greater cooperation among agencies and units of local government, clearer objectives and priorities, more effective resource allocation, and better quality criminal justice programs and personnel. Taken together, these results can increase public confidence in and support for criminal justice processes, enhancing system performance and, ultimately, the integrity of the law.

Improved planning and coordination help individual justice agencies become more efficient, productive, and effective. Such improvements also help officials of general government—such as the city mayor, board of supervisors, and county commissioners—evaluate and make decisions about the justice system and its cost and performance. Many local governments also are finding that comprehensive systemwide planning (interagency and cross-jurisdictional) helps to streamline the entire local system of justice, eliminating duplication, filling service gaps, and generally improving the quality of service while controlling costs.

The major benefits of local justice planning are shown in the following exhibit, which illustrates the relationships between major planning activities and lists goals and objectives that could be adopted by any CJCC.

Guide Overview

Section 1 of this guide addresses the need for improved justice system coordination. It describes the connections between planning, analysis, and coordination; summarizes the benefits of local justice planning and coordination; and discusses the context within which coordination must be achieved. This section also contains a questionnaire for a quick self-evaluation that may be conducted by any jurisdiction.

Section 2 establishes a justice planning and coordination framework designed to provide a better understanding of the planning process as a discipline. It begins by describing planning and coor-

dination efforts at three levels: the justice *agency* level; the *city/county* level; and the *comprehensive* interagency and intergovernmental level, where planning and coordination are focused on the justice system as a whole. This section of the guide emphasizes comprehensive planning and coordination. It describes a collaborative method for improving systemwide coordination, one that abandons reliance on centralized planning and

Activities, Objectives, Purpose, and Goals of Local Justice Planning

Major Justice Planning Activities

• Crime analysis • Criminal justice system analysis • Productivity analysis • Legislative analysis • Special studies • Database development	• Definition of responsibilities • Convening and serving coordinating groups • Coordination with other planning units	• Formulation of goal statements • Clarification of issues and values • Construction of goal hierarchies	• Management of federal/ state/local resources • Review of agency budgets	• Program design, development, implementation, and evaluation	• Technical assistance • Information brokerage

Planning Objectives

Improved analysis of criminal justice problems	Improved coordination and cooperation	Clearer goals, objectives, and priorities	More effective allocation of resources	Improved criminal justice programs and services	Improved capacity and quality of personnel

Purpose of Planning

Improved criminal justice policy, program, and operational decisionmaking

Criminal Justice System Goals

Protect integrity of the law	Control crime and delinquency and/ or root out causes of crime	Improve quality of justice	Improve criminal justice system and related programs	Increase community support for criminal justice system

control. The approach set forth protects and honors the independence of elected and appointed officials from the different branches and levels of government.

Section 2 also describes three *types* of planning: policy, program, and operational. It shows how these types of planning can be linked systematically in a series of planning steps to improve justice system communication, cooperation, and coordination. Exhibits 3, 4, and 5 illustrate how policy planning (setting goals and objectives) leads to program planning (selecting specific courses of action), which then leads to operational planning (allocating resources to implement plans). Evaluation of the planning process feeds knowledge into a new planning cycle. Such step-by-step planning can lead to incremental improvement in justice system operations.

Identifying and analyzing problems is one of the most important steps in the planning process. For this reason, this guide offers concrete examples that demonstrate the critical role of data collection and analysis. It also describes how CJCCs convert data into useful information.

Section 3 describes distinctive coordination mechanisms that improve local justice system collaboration. Each represents an increasingly more comprehensive coordination model—an evolution toward an ideal CJCC.

Section 4 prescribes guidelines and principles for creating, staffing, evaluating, rejuvenating, and demonstrating the benefits of a CJCC.

Examples from local jurisdictions with advanced planning practices are provided throughout the guide. These illustrate how the planning process is being applied to improve justice coordination throughout the United States. This guide also includes five appendixes:

- **Appendix A** provides a checklist for forming or rejuvenating a CJCC.

- **Appendix B** lists the jurisdictions mentioned in this guide.

- **Appendix C** lists CJCC resources.

- **Appendix D** provides a sample charge for a criminal justice task force.

- **Appendix E** provides sample bylaws for a CJCC.

Introduction

> *If you don't know where you're going, you might end up somewhere else.*
>
> —Casey Stengel[1]

This guide is designed to help local government officials improve justice planning, analysis, and coordination capabilities. It responds to a need identified by National Institute of Corrections (NIC) consultants who have been providing onsite technical assistance to local governments throughout the United States. They report that many of the corrections-related issues that trigger requests for technical assistance are rooted in underdeveloped local justice system planning, analysis, and coordination capabilities.

Jail crowding and planning for new facilities frequently result in requests for technical assistance from NIC. In these situations, weak local planning, analysis, and justice system coordination are special handicaps. These capabilities are essential if a community is to manage its way out of its current situation successfully. Improving a local government's abilities in these areas offers benefits far beyond improved management of problems at the jail or corrections in general. This guide will help any community improve its justice *system* (that is, the way all of the justice agencies within a local jurisdiction work together).

A criminal justice coordinating committee (CJCC), or a similarly constituted group, is the key mechanism for accomplishing these improvements. "Criminal justice coordinating committee" is an inclusive term applied to informal and formal committees that provide forums in which a large number of key justice system agency officials and other officials of general government may discuss justice system issues.

Although it may not be apparent at first, planning demonstrates an optimistic attitude. It reflects the point of view that citizens, as well as appointed and elected officials, can change the way things work instead of being victimized by circumstances that appear to be beyond their control.

This guide offers advice on how CJCCs can be initiated within local governments, describes the range of planning and coordinating activities that might be undertaken, describes alternative organizational forms for CJCCs, presents guidelines for operating a CJCC, and describes the benefits local governments can expect to derive from these activities.

The CJCC has many variations but often evolves into the ideal, formalized structure associated with its name. The challenge for local governments is to fashion their own "localized" approach; this guide is designed to help achieve that goal. (See appendixes A through C for a checklist of items to consider when forming or reviving a CJCC; a list of jurisdictions mentioned in this guide; and a list of other training and technical assistance resources, information resources, and free publications available to jurisdictions considering establishing a CJCC.)

CJCC Self-Evaluation Questionnaire

Exhibit 1 is a questionnaire that will permit jurisdictions to conduct a quick self-evaluation. Any local jurisdiction that can answer all of these questions in the affirmative has a healthy CJCC and probably is achieving competent systemwide planning and coordination. Jurisdictions seeking to improve their CJCCs can do so by implementing many of the suggestions set forth in this guide.

Exhibit 1. CJCC Self-Evaluation Questionnaire					
	Score 1=no or never; 5=yes or always				
1. Does the CJCC deal with a complete or nearly complete local justice system? (Do all local programs and services for offenders fall within the planning jurisdiction?)	1	2	3	4	5
2. Does the CJCC have sufficient authority to obtain necessary data and to develop plans for the local justice system? (Is the CJCC formally authorized to undertake comprehensive systemwide planning and coordination? Does it have adequate access to agency information, and do agencies cooperate in implementing plans?)	1	2	3	4	5
3. Is planning well integrated into the operations of general government? (Does the CJCC receive significant financial support or other support from the local government?)	1	2	3	4	5
4. Does the CJCC emphasize policy- and program-level planning (as compared with being preoccupied with operational planning)?	1	2	3	4	5
5. Are the CJCC members attending meetings? (Is attendance good? Do the members, rather than alternates, frequently attend?)	1	2	3	4	5
6. Does the CJCC undertake a wide variety of activities rather than allocate grant funds?	1	2	3	4	5
7. Is the CJCC broadly representative (e.g., city/county/state/federal levels of government; executive/judicial/legislative branches; law enforcement, courts; corrections subsystems; other major constituencies)?	1	2	3	4	5
8. Does the CJCC have sufficient, independent staff support?	1	2	3	4	5
9. Is sufficient attention devoted to planning for planning? (Have policymakers thought out exactly what they want the CJCC to accomplish and how these goals will be achieved? Are planning tasks clearly delineated? Have staff been recruited with the skills and experience needed to undertake these tasks? Have the duties, responsibilities, and functions of the CJCC been specified and communicated to participating agencies?)	1	2	3	4	5
10. Do neutrality, credibility, and stability characterize the CJCC? (Can agency personnel trust the chair, executive committee, and staff to remain impartial and to act in the interest of the system as a whole? Does the staff facilitate good working relationships with agency personnel and other officials of local government?)	1	2	3	4	5
11. Have the CJCC and its planning process been systematically evaluated? Do the evaluation results demonstrate the CJCC's usefulness to local government?	1	2	3	4	5

The Need for Improved Criminal Justice Coordination

In most jurisdictions of the United States, the responsibility for crime prevention, crime control, and improvement of the administration of justice rests largely with local government. But often, the local government machinery set up to deal with crime does not work well. Examples may include the following:

• The narcotics detail of a police department postpones arrests until the entire network of a drug ring is identified, then processes 50 to 100 new cases into the local justice system. Jails and courts, unprepared for the influx, are suddenly more crowded and backlogged.

• In another locale, the jail has been crowded for a long time, the county cannot afford to build a new one, and public support for financing a new jail is at an all-time low. Legal liability is a concern, yet officials of general government and justice agencies seem to be immobilized. There is no consensus about what needs to be done.

• Concerned about crime, a county board of commissioners approves a large budget increase for county law enforcement and jails. Increasing the capacities of only part of the system, however, results in more arrests for minor offenses, increases the jail population, and contributes to court delay but does not reduce serious crime.

Situations like these are familiar in many localities. The first indication that a major decision has been made in one part of the criminal justice system often comes in the form of a deluge of new cases that overwhelms another part of the system. Agencies needlessly duplicate each other's efforts, increasing the overall cost of local services. Decisions made with inadequate information produce unintended or unanticipated effects. Interagency disputes may be settled only when the opposing parties tire of fighting.

The Connection Between Planning, Analysis, and Coordination

Planning is the process by which we bring anticipations of the future to bear on current decisionmaking. Planning is future oriented, rooted in the belief that we can make decisions that not only will help us anticipate and cope with alternative futures but also will help us have more control over determining that future.

> *"Would you tell me, please, which way I ought to walk from here?" asked Alice. "That depends a good deal on where you want to get to," said the Cheshire Cat. "I don't much care where—" said Alice. "Then it doesn't matter which way you go," said the Cat. "— so long as I get somewhere," Alice added as an explanation. "Oh, you're sure to do that," said the Cat, "if you only walk long enough."*
>
> **—Lewis Carroll,**
> ***Alice's Adventures in Wonderland***[2]

Planning is an integral part of informed policy making and competent agency management. Because planning involves defining problems, clarifying objectives, establishing priorities, and instituting programs, every executive must regard planning as a major responsibility of his or her job. Planning is part of the executive function, not something to be assigned to others.

Local justice planning is directed toward the goal of improved decisionmaking. It *requires* analysis and *produces* improved coordination as well as other benefits. Planning is the larger concept. Interestingly, the words "planning," "analysis," and "coordination" are often used interchangeably, as if it is understood that they are related. More recently, the word "collaboration" has often been substituted for the word "coordination."

> *More recent definitions of comprehensive criminal justice planning have taken on the meaning of planning as coordination. This recognizes that fragmentation is a fact in the criminal justice system and that decisionmaking is decentralized. Central planning as a comprehensive model tends to be associated with total control, and this runs counter to the separation of powers doctrine.*
>
> **—Christina Morehead,**
> ***A Criminal Justice Planning Model for King County***[3]

Over the years, criminal justice planning committees increasingly have been renamed "criminal justice coordinating committees." This change reflects a realistic attempt to move away from some negative baggage associated with the word "planning," especially its connection to centralization of authority and control. Centralization of control is an unfortunate feature of some planning efforts. It offends independently elected and appointed officials who feel obligated to constantly fight against erosion of their authority. So, to many, a criminal justice *coordinating* committee may initially appear to be a criminal justice *planning* committee in disguise.

This guide attempts to assuage these fears by describing a collaborative version of planning that is devoid of emphasis on controlling others.

But the issue will most likely resurface in each locality that attempts even the collaborative version of planning being recommended here.

> *We face an inescapable choice between planning and chaos.*
>
> —**Norman Bel Geddes**

Benefits of Local Justice Planning and Coordination

Good planning at the local level can be expected to result in:

- **Improved analysis of problems.** Planning produces the data and analyses needed by elected officials and justice administrators to improve their decisionmaking.

- **Improved communication, cooperation, and coordination.** Planning provides a mechanism for improving communication, cooperation, and coordination among police, courts, corrections, and private service agencies as well as between different levels of government and the three branches of government. Improved coordination is a *result* of planning.

- **Clear goals, objectives, and priorities.** Planning permits more precise articulation of purposes and links goals, objectives, tasks, and activities in more meaningful ways.

- **More effective allocation of resources.** Planning provides a framework for resource allocation decisions. It simplifies setting priorities for the use of resources to achieve justice goals and objectives.

- **Improved programs and services.** Planning produces a clearer understanding of problems and needs. Planning also makes it easier to formulate goals and objectives and to evaluate and compare alternative programs and procedures.

- **Improved capacity and quality of personnel.** Planning focuses organizational effort and provides agency personnel with new knowledge and information.

Planning can result in benefits to the entire community, such as making the justice system more accountable, more open to the public, more efficient, and more effective. Justice system coordination can also save taxpayer money.

> *Systemwide planning affords an opportunity for the disparate components of the justice structure to work together. Collaboration in the analysis of problems and the sharing of information, resources, and expertise can build local capacity for crime prevention, justice reform, and community mobilization. Strong planning capacity can also provide elected officials and criminal justice executives with the data and analysis essential for establishing rational policies and priorities for a complex system.*
>
> —**Christina Morehead,**
> ***A Criminal Justice Planning Model for King County***[4]

Many different justice planning and coordination activities serve to improve justice system policy, program, and operational decisionmaking at the local level. Exhibit 2 illustrates the relationships between major classes of justice planning activities and general objectives and goals that may be adopted by any CJCC. Each planning activity contributes to one or more of the six planning objectives, which, in turn, contribute to improved decisionmaking and, ultimately, to the achievement of justice system goals. Although most planning activities actually contribute to the achievement of more than one planning objective, each is located above the one it most directly serves.

Planning can also increase public confidence in and support for the justice system. Ultimately, the effectiveness of the justice system depends on the willingness of the majority of citizens to obey the law and to report crime, identify suspects, and cooperate with the prosecution. Citizen cooperation is also necessary if ex-offenders are to reintegrate into the fabric of the community successfully. Anything that can be done to increase

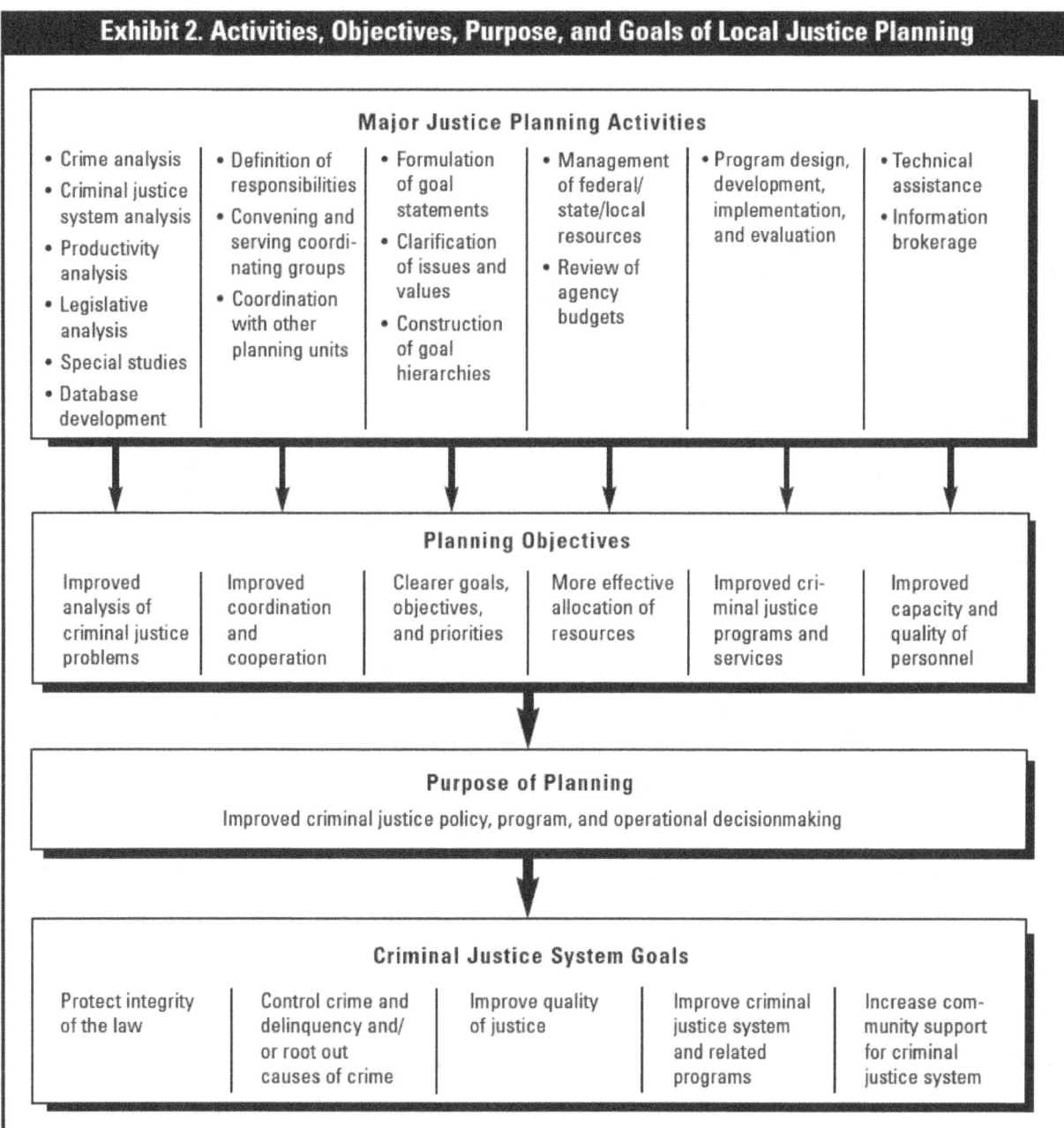

Exhibit 2. Activities, Objectives, Purpose, and Goals of Local Justice Planning

Major Justice Planning Activities

- Crime analysis
- Criminal justice system analysis
- Productivity analysis
- Legislative analysis
- Special studies
- Database development

- Definition of responsibilities
- Convening and serving coordinating groups
- Coordination with other planning units

- Formulation of goal statements
- Clarification of issues and values
- Construction of goal hierarchies

- Management of federal/state/local resources
- Review of agency budgets

- Program design, development, implementation, and evaluation

- Technical assistance
- Information brokerage

Planning Objectives

| Improved analysis of criminal justice problems | Improved coordination and cooperation | Clearer goals, objectives, and priorities | More effective allocation of resources | Improved criminal justice programs and services | Improved capacity and quality of personnel |

Purpose of Planning

Improved criminal justice policy, program, and operational decisionmaking

Criminal Justice System Goals

| Protect integrity of the law | Control crime and delinquency and/or root out causes of crime | Improve quality of justice | Improve criminal justice system and related programs | Increase community support for criminal justice system |

public confidence in the justice system and its support for justice processes contributes to system performance. A coherent plan, produced by a coordinating body that speaks with a responsible voice, can soothe public fears of crime and allay any concerns that little can be done about it.

In the aggregate, planning can protect the integrity of the law. Planning can produce a justice system

that makes it unnecessary for aggrieved citizens to take the law into their own hands; that does not allow the morale of justice agency personnel to sink to the point where unethical behavior seems justified; and that prevents public services from becoming so poor that courts must close facilities and grand juries must expose scandals. As people recognize that crime is less a problem to be solved than a condition to be managed, planning is increasingly viewed as a sign of good management. Planning protects the integrity of the law to the degree that it converts ideals into practice—by administering justice. Competent planning, in short, is a sign of good government.

Effective collaboration also protects the leaders essential to successful change. All public system reform requires risk taking on the part of its leaders. The justice system operates in a politically charged environment. . . . Maintaining the status quo is much easier and certainly the path of least resistance. It is safer, but it is sometimes wrong . . . but no leader can or should be expected to bear all the risks. A collaborative body involving all the system's actors provides a context for leadership to emerge and offers the protection of collegial support and policy consensus when controversy—a predictable by-product of real change—eventually arises.

—**Kathleen Feely,** *Collaboration and Leadership in Juvenile Detention Reform*[5]

The Context of Planning and Coordination

Developing competence in planning and applying it effectively to criminal justice policymaking and operations is no easy task. In large part, the difficulties of justice planning (as well as the need for it) arise from the nature of the system itself. By design, the system is fragmented. No central authority manages it. No one branch of government or level of government is responsible for the entire process.

The checks and balances with which the local justice system is punctuated are intentional and necessary, but they do result in inefficiencies and conflicts. There is great dispersion of power

among divergent forces. And the professional orientations, values, and managerial perspectives of key agency participants are markedly different—often diametrically opposed. This makes conflict and tension among justice agencies virtually inevitable as each understandably attempts to turn events to its own advantage.

Appointed and elected officials of general government and citizens concerned with broad policy issues must rely on justice agency heads for advice on what to do about crime and justice problems. But these executives seldom agree. Although the different agencies must interact (they share the same clients and workload), they often do so only when absolutely necessary—and then with little apparent concern for the "system" of which they are a part.

Typically, policing is a city function, while the courts are state, the prosecutor independent whether he is city, county or state, and corrections divided between the city or county jail function and the state prison. Typically, three levels of government are also involved—city, county, and state—as well as two branches of government—executive and judicial—with involvement as well on policy and funding matters by the legislative branch. Throughout the system, many officials are directly elected, and therefore even if they are performing what is normally regarded as an executive function, they are likely to be independent of the chief executive of the jurisdiction.

—**Blair Ewing,** former Policy Adviser, U.S. Department of Justice[6]

In such a context, comprehensive planning must seek to build linkages among agency decisionmakers without attempting to subordinate them to any higher authority. No one is at the helm, but no "master planner" will be allowed to steer. Not fragmentation, but the problems resulting from it, must be the target. Accommodation and cooperation can be fostered only if planning is able to demonstrate mutual regard for agencies that work together to achieve shared objectives. The independence of the key participants must be respected.

The justice system is like a large plumbing apparatus, held together only by the material flowing through it.

—**Richard A. McGee, former Administrator, Youth and Adult Corrections Agency, State of California**

Sometimes, a concern about respecting the doctrine of the separation of powers leads a key justice leader, often a judge, to express discomfort at being asked to serve on a CJCC. But judges serve on many CJCCs and, in fact, chair them in some communities.

The reality is that CJCCs bring independently elected and appointed people together in a forum

---

All of us have this concept that we know what each other does. I've learned that I haven't a clue about what other people do and the problems that they have and how what we do may affect them. Only when you understand them can you give them due consideration. If you can accommodate them, then you do.

—**Adjudication partnership member, quoted in Jane Nady Sigmon et al., *Adjudication Partnerships: Critical Components***[7]

---

where they agree to work together, realizing they have interdependent relationships. Under the constitutions of each state, these key participants recognize they are independent and have an obligation to remain so. Nothing in this model should be interpreted to suggest that they will or should lose their independence.

A Framework for Justice Planning and Coordination

Justice planning is a discipline that may be applied at the agency, city/county, and comprehensive systemwide levels to improve decisionmaking in three broad areas. The three types of planning (policy, program, and operational) are described in this section, and an 11-step general model of the planning process is presented. Problem identification and analysis, a critical planning step, is given special emphasis.

Levels of Planning and Coordination: Agency, City/County, and Comprehensive

More advanced local planning and coordination efforts are able to link local justice planning, and therefore local decisionmaking, at three levels of government: the justice agency level, the city/county level, and the local justice system level. All three levels of planning are important, and each strengthens and receives support from the others. But the purpose and emphasis at the three levels are not the same.

Agency Planning and Coordination

At the agency level, planning is designed to assist top management of a department or agency—the police chief, sheriff, or chief judge. Planning at this level should be targeted toward the needs of the agency and the decisions it must regularly make. Agency planners will develop statistical analyses to support administrative and operational decisions; review, update, and disseminate policies, procedures, rules, and regulations; and assist in the preparation of agency budgets. Agency planning is aided by planning at the city, county, and interagency levels, and it contributes to planning at more comprehensive levels.

City/County Planning and Coordination

At the city/county level, the individual justice agency heads are joined by officials of general government—the mayor, city council, city and county chief administrative officers, county commissioners—and the planning and coordination efforts shift to meet the decisionmaking needs of these officials as well.

Coordinated city/county planning requires cooperation to integrate the efforts of autonomous criminal justice agencies, each with their own mandates, perspectives, and constituencies. At the county level, for example, local justice planning might mean coordinating the activities of the county sheriff, the probation department, the prosecutor, the public defender, and the county courts. The challenge at this level is to enhance cooperation and coordination among constitutionally separate government agencies. Such interagency planning both contributes to and is advanced by the planning of individual agencies and more comprehensive justice systemwide planning and coordination.

Comprehensive Systemwide Justice Planning and Coordination

There is also a need for local planning at a third level—the comprehensive set of police, court, corrections, and allied public and private agencies that make up the criminal justice system. Separate planning efforts at the city/county level are limited in their ability to deal with the total justice system because neither jurisdiction contains all the components of that system. At a minimum, comprehensive planning and coordination must join city/county efforts and deal with the individual responsibilities of police, courts, and corrections agencies. But it may extend even farther. Planning and coordination at this systemwide level may require coordination of city, county, regional, state, federal, and private justice agency activities. It also may involve organizations other than criminal justice agencies (e.g., public assistance agencies, employment agencies, and the schools) that provide services to offenders. This type of planning, then, transcends jurisdictional and agency boundaries.

> *To be really effective, local criminal justice planning must encompass all three levels— justice agency planning, coordinated justice planning on a citywide and countywide basis, and comprehensive planning for the local justice system as a whole. The three levels are interdependent building blocks of local planning. Each has its own purposes and distinguishing characteristics, but planning at all three levels of government should interlock.*
>
> —**Robert C. Cushman**[a]

Policy, Program, and Operational Planning

Justice planning is concerned with improving decisionmaking in three broad areas: (1) the identification of long-term goals and objectives (policy planning), (2) the selection of specific courses of action (program planning), and (3) the allocation of resources to accomplish defined purposes (operational planning). Relationships among these three levels of planning are illustrated in exhibit 3.

Policy Planning

Policy planning is focused on answering the question, What should we do and why? It produces policy guidelines expressing important values, philosophies, and judgments on which to base long-term plans. Thus, policy planning leads to decisions that determine long-term justice goals and objectives.

Program Planning

Program planning is designed to answer the question, What can we do and how? It is concerned

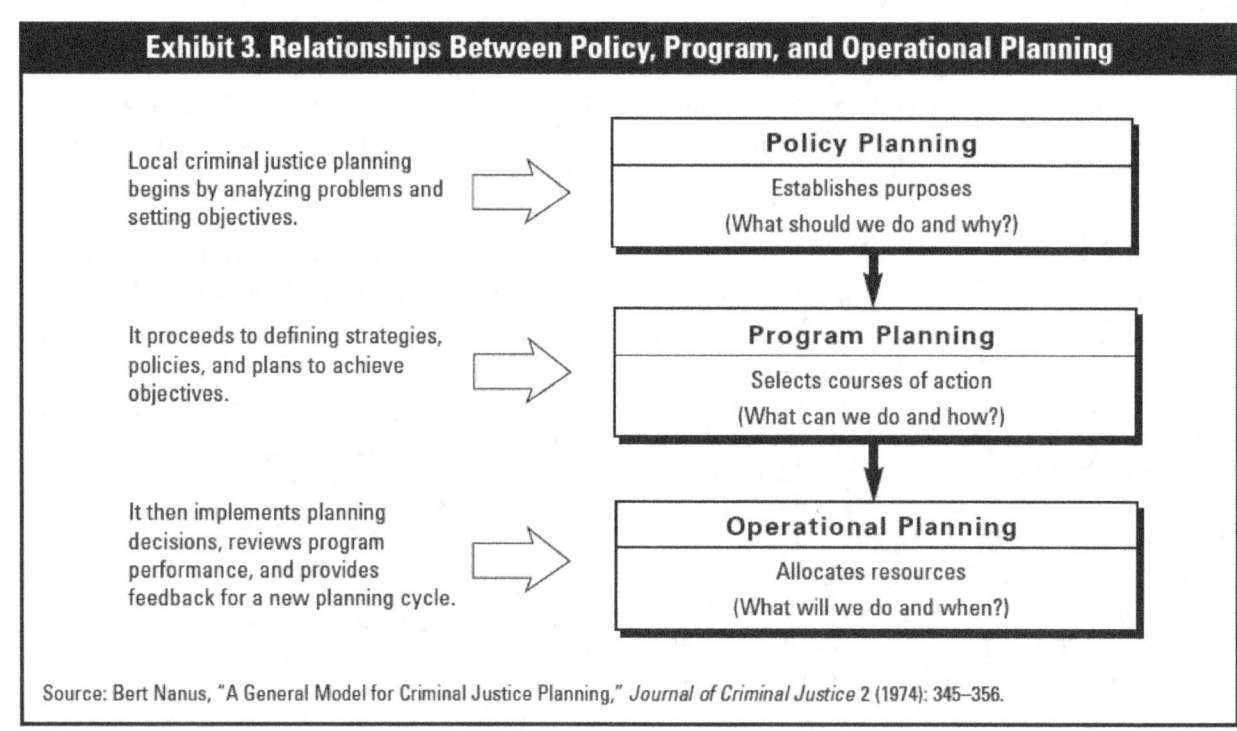

Exhibit 3. Relationships Between Policy, Program, and Operational Planning

Local criminal justice planning begins by analyzing problems and setting objectives.
→
Policy Planning
Establishes purposes
(What should we do and why?)

It proceeds to defining strategies, policies, and plans to achieve objectives.
→
Program Planning
Selects courses of action
(What can we do and how?)

It then implements planning decisions, reviews program performance, and provides feedback for a new planning cycle.
→
Operational Planning
Allocates resources
(What will we do and when?)

Source: Bert Nanus, "A General Model for Criminal Justice Planning," *Journal of Criminal Justice* 2 (1974): 345–356.

with assessing the feasibility of alternative courses of action, developing appropriate program and contingency plans, and constructing guidelines for action. Thus, program planning decisions lead to the adoption of specific courses of action.

Operational Planning

Operational planning answers the question, What will we do and when? It produces specific plans for the allocation of resources to implement and evaluate justice programs and services. Thus, operational planning decisions lead to the allocation of resources to implement plans. Examples

of activities associated with these three levels of planning are presented in exhibit 4.

Reactive Decisionmaking

Policy, program, and operational planning contrast with reactive decisionmaking, which can be destructive to any organization. Reactive decisionmaking is largely unplanned and crisis oriented. It often involves prompt mobilization of large numbers of justice agency and general government personnel. A certain amount of reactive decisionmaking takes place in most agencies and government units. In some, it is the primary mode

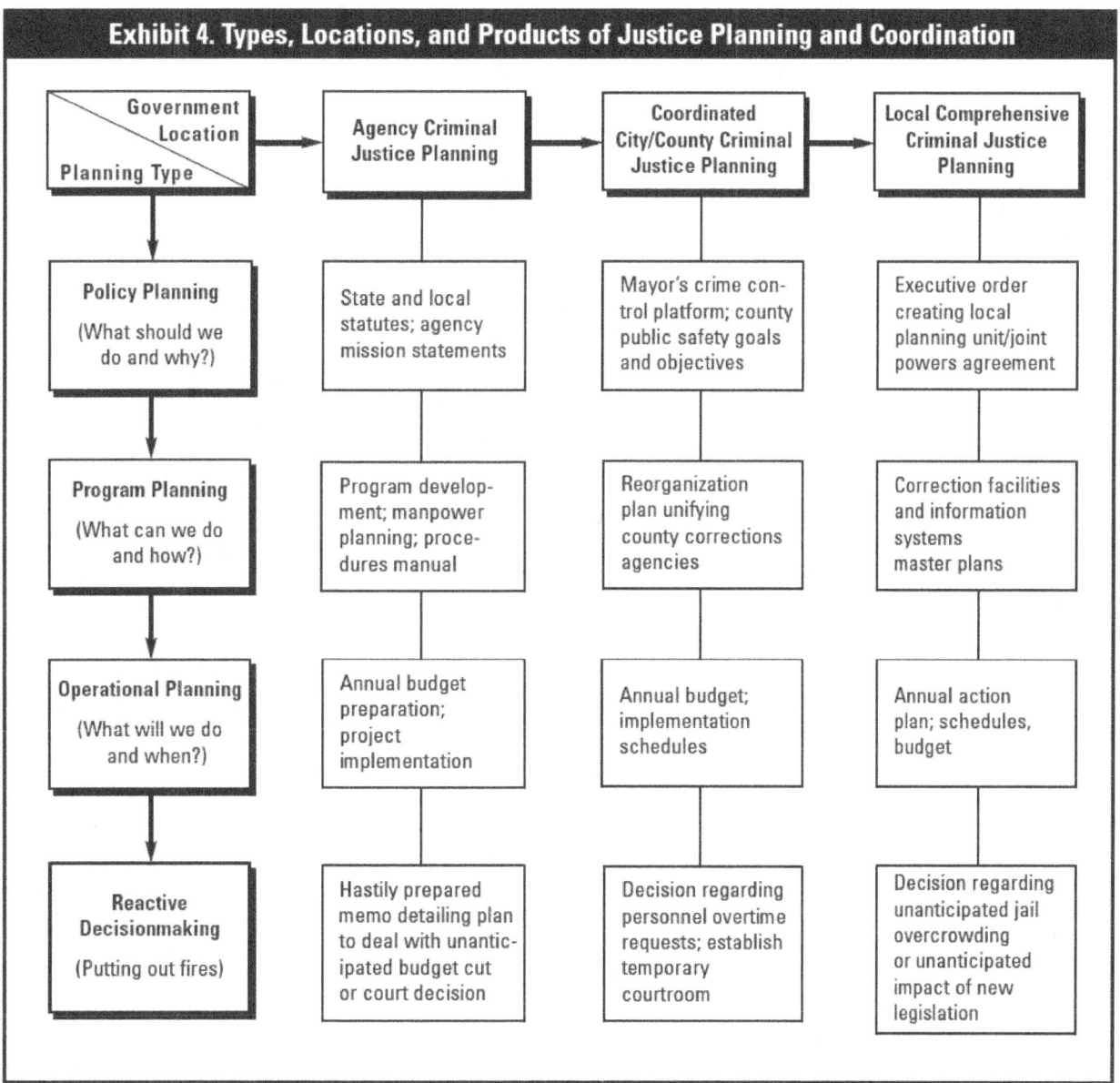

Exhibit 4. Types, Locations, and Products of Justice Planning and Coordination

Government Location / Planning Type	Agency Criminal Justice Planning	Coordinated City/County Criminal Justice Planning	Local Comprehensive Criminal Justice Planning
Policy Planning (What should we do and why?)	State and local statutes; agency mission statements	Mayor's crime control platform; county public safety goals and objectives	Executive order creating local planning unit/joint powers agreement
Program Planning (What can we do and how?)	Program development; manpower planning; procedures manual	Reorganization plan unifying county corrections agencies	Correction facilities and information systems master plans
Operational Planning (What will we do and when?)	Annual budget preparation; project implementation	Annual budget; implementation schedules	Annual action plan; schedules, budget
Reactive Decisionmaking (Putting out fires)	Hastily prepared memo detailing plan to deal with unanticipated budget cut or court decision	Decision regarding personnel overtime requests; establish temporary courtroom	Decision regarding unanticipated jail overcrowding or unanticipated impact of new legislation

for the day-to-day management of immediate organizational problems. Such a "firefighting" approach can be disruptive. Examples of reactive decisionmaking are also shown in exhibit 4. Planning can help reduce the need for this kind of crisis-oriented decisionmaking.

Reactive decisionmaking administers first aid. It is not designed to produce lasting solutions. In fact, the amount of time and energy expended on reactive decisionmaking is one measure of an organization's inability to anticipate and affect its own future.

—Billy Wasson, former Staff Director, Marion County (Oregon) Public Safety Coordinating Council

---

Policy, program, and operational planning and coordination flow together in practice. Each type of planning should take place at each planning level. It would be a mistake to assume, for example, that the federal government does policy planning while state governments do program planning and local governments do operational planning.

Today, in most jurisdictions, the need to respond to short-term workload crises, immediate political events, and a 1-year budget cycle encourages a focus on operational planning and the allocation of resources. As a result, personnel spend a disproportionate amount of time and effort on operational planning at the expense of policy and program planning. Experience has shown that, for policy and program planning to occur, they must be deliberately, consciously, and continuously emphasized by top management. Policymakers must insist on it, and staff resources assigned to these functions must be protected from being diverted back into operational planning.

A General Model of the Planning Process

A rational planning model can lead to a more balanced focus on policy, program, and operational planning. There are many planning models. Most

consist of an orderly series of interdependent steps and follow a rather predictable path from policy planning through program and operational planning. One general planning model, consisting of 11 steps, is shown in exhibit 5.

In this model, policy planning begins with preparing for planning (step 1), followed by efforts to forecast probable, possible, and desirable future states (steps 2 through 4). Program planning includes efforts to identify problems (step 5), set goals (step 6), identify alternative courses of action (step 7), and select preferred alternatives (step 8). Operational planning (steps 9 through 11) includes planning for implementation, implementing plans, and monitoring and evaluating progress. The final step, monitoring and evaluation (step 11), provides the feedback needed to improve decisionmaking each time the full planning cycle takes place. Each level of government needs to adopt its own version of such a step-by-step planning process. Jurisdictions with advanced practices use some version of this process to guide local justice planning.

Key decisionmakers not attending your CJCC meetings? Are they sending alternates or not appearing at all? Solution: Make sure policy matters are at the core of the agenda and discussion. The policymakers will attend.

—Mark Cunniff, Executive Director, National Association of Criminal Justice Planners

---

Improved Understanding of Justice Problems

The limited scope of this guide does not permit a thorough description of each of the planning steps shown in exhibit 5 or the major planning activities shown in exhibit 2. Nevertheless, it is necessary to discuss certain activities that contribute to improved analysis of justice problems.

The ability to conduct analyses is at the heart of the problem identification step (step 5) of the

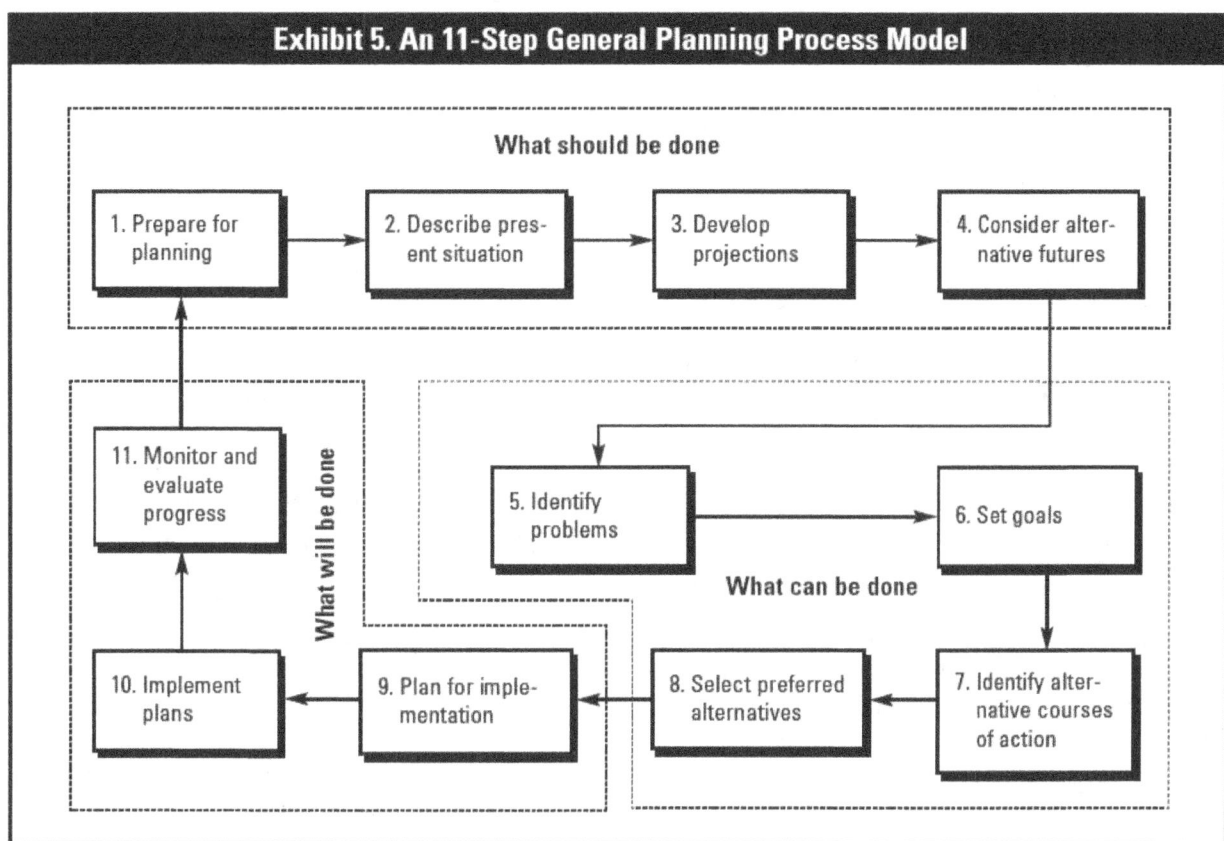

Exhibit 5. An 11-Step General Planning Process Model

What should be done

1. Prepare for planning → 2. Describe present situation → 3. Develop projections → 4. Consider alternative futures

What will be done

11. Monitor and evaluate progress

5. Identify problems → 6. Set goals

What can be done

10. Implement plans ← 9. Plan for implementation ← 8. Select preferred alternatives ← 7. Identify alternative courses of action

---

11-step general planning process model. Without a clear analysis of problems, many justice decisions are guided solely by past experience, anecdotes that describe atypical cases, intuition, and conflicting testimonies.

Development of effective criminal justice policy is rooted in the ability of a jurisdiction to obtain data on how its system operates and the ability to analyze that data and present that data in a meaningful manner.

—Kim Allen, former Executive Director, Louisville-Jefferson County (Kentucky) Crime Commission[9]

The Critical Role of Information

Competent planning produces the information needed by local officials and agency executives to improve their understanding of justice problems.

A constant flow of timely and relevant information helps decisionmakers define justice problems, set goals and priorities, and implement and evaluate strategies for accomplishing goals. It provides managers with new facts and new knowledge, in a cumulative fashion. It sets the stage for a continuous improvement process built on knowledge that can replace the trial-and-error method of initiating programs.

Development of an Adequate Database

Because basic information needed for decisionmaking is lacking in most jurisdictions, most CJCCs must concentrate first on the development of an adequate database. Problems in accessing data generated by justice agencies must be overcome. If enabling legislation does not formally provide for access to data, the CJCC leadership must work to establish the relationships and informal understandings that will ensure such access.

> *Experience in many local jurisdictions has shown that these problems can be overcome by providing an adequate information base for use in the analysis of crime and criminal justice problems. This puts local government in a better position to base actions upon knowledge gained.*
>
> **—Brian Mattson, Criminal Justice Planner, Jefferson County (Colorado) Criminal Justice Coordination Committee**

Early emphasis should also be given to describing system operations and identifying problems. Constructing clear statements of problems and setting objectives for overcoming them will help direct the planning effort toward solving specific problems. A problem-solving orientation also will help galvanize organizational action around visible, concrete, and attainable objectives and give plans greater relevance, credibility, and substance.

Integration of Data From Disparate Information Systems

Although most jurisdictions have a large amount of data, they often do not have the ability to convert that data into useful information. CJCCs often take on the challenge of integrating disparate justice information systems. For example, the Hennepin County/City of Minneapolis CJCC created a subcommittee—the Integrated Systems Advisory Board—and assigned the board responsibility for developing a business model for integrating the criminal justice information systems at the city, county, and state levels. A number of CJCCs took this same approach, including those in Sacramento and Los Angeles Counties, California; Lucas County, Ohio; and Westchester County, New York.

At the core of Decision Support System-Justice in Multnomah County, Oregon, is a "data warehouse," a large centralized database that integrates selected data from a variety of local and state criminal justice agencies. Los Angeles County has

adopted a similar approach. Other communities have developed "subject in process" information systems that track individual offenders from arrest to final disposition.

Overcoming Common Problems in Conducting an Analysis

Four problems are commonly found in jurisdictions where analysis capability is inadequate or absent: the crime problem has not been defined, a comparative context cannot be established, there is an inability to define problems at key system decision points in the criminal justice process, and incomplete analysis has been conducted.

Crime Problem Not Defined

The first area of concern is a lack of reliable and sufficiently detailed statistics to clearly define the crime problem—statistics concerning the offender, the victim, the criminal event, and the environment in which the crime occurs. When the CJCC conducts a crime analysis, it will acquire detailed information describing criminal events, offenders, and victims. Usually, this can be accomplished by analyzing data that already exist in police offense reports, arrest reports, and dispatch cards.

Comparative Context Cannot Be Established

The second common problem is that the jurisdiction has not developed and assessed data that will allow it to compare itself with other jurisdictions of similar size and circumstance. The data usually are available, but a comparative analysis has never been constructed. A simple comparative analysis compares a county with perhaps four or five counties in the state that are somewhat smaller in population and another four or five counties that are somewhat larger. Other statewide averages (e.g., mean and median scores) might also be included.

This information can be produced in tabular form as shown in exhibit 6, which shows scores for each county along with an average for the 8 to 10 other counties (a composite or surrogate peer county average). It shows the percent difference between the jurisdiction and this average. This type of analysis will provide any jurisdiction with a useful comparative context.

The comparative analysis tables should contain rates per 10,000 population for the following measures:

• Crimes reported to the police, including separate calculations for violent and nonviolent crime.

• Adult and juvenile arrests for felonies and misdemeanors.

• Number of felony, misdemeanor, and traffic filings and dispositions in local and state courts.

• Number of jail bookings for felony, misdemeanor, and traffic law violations, by arresting agency.

• Average length of jail stay, by type of inmate.

• Average daily population in jail, by inmate type.

• Number of people on felony and misdemeanor probation.

• Commitments to state prison.

Similar indicators and measures can also be collected concerning the processing of juvenile cases.

A subsequent step in this analysis is to develop a picture of current *trends* within the jurisdiction, using these same crime and justice workload items. Here, the comparison is not with other counties but, rather, is a year-to-year comparison of changes within the jurisdiction over time (perhaps a 5-year period). This will help inform the jurisdiction about trends and changes in the local justice system.

Inability to Define Problems at Key System Decision Points

The third area of concern is a lack of meaningful statistics and information to describe and define problems in the criminal justice process. The

Exhibit 6. Comparative Analysis Example

County	County Population (1999)	Serious Crimes Reported to Police	Serious Crime Rate (per 10,000 population)
A	45,164	1,896	417.6
B	43,430	1,925	443.2
C	40,281	1,780	441.9
D	39,595	2,106	531.9
E	36,572	3,254	889.8
F	36,427	1,327	364.3
G	35,886	1,431	398.8
H	35,636	1,882	528.1
Peer county total			501.95
County of interest	38,900	1,732	445.2
Percent difference			−11.3

Note: This is an example of only a few of the items that could appear in a comparative analysis. Other statewide averages could also be added to the table (e.g., statewide mean or statewide median scores).

remedy here is to initiate a justice system analysis to produce detailed and comprehensive statistics about the workings of the criminal justice system.

Usually a flow chart is constructed to show the number of persons and cases entering the justice system and the processes that lead to final disposition. Creating a flow chart in itself informs analysis by describing more precisely the justice system and its boundaries and illustrating the interdependencies among system components. The level of detail depends on the purpose of the analysis and the data available, but even the simplest flow chart can provide a useful snapshot of the justice system in operation.

The seven key justice system decision points to be shown in the flow chart include:

- The decision to arrest.

- The decision to detain pretrial.

- The decision to release from pretrial detention.

- The decision to prosecute.

- The adjudication decision.

- The sentencing decision.

- The decision to modify a sentence.

The flow chart will represent offender and case flow, as shown in exhibit 7. This is a justice "system" representation.

One advantage of a justice system analysis is that it minimizes the need to identify problems associated with individual agencies. It is centered on analyzing *processes* (i.e., on analyzing the decision points in the system where the agencies come together to do their work).

The flow of cases and people through the seven justice system decision points is governed by justice policies, which are subject to change. Changes in policy have workload and expenditure impacts. The data provide an empirical picture of current policies and begin to identify policy choice alternatives.

A metaphor for the analysis process involves shining a light on each decision point to illuminate it. Once illuminated, the data that empirically describe current policy can be mirrored back—not only to justice system decisionmakers but also to other justice system officials who may be affected by the existing policies and to officials of general government and the public. Often, changes occur as a result of this feedback process alone. No other action is necessary.

All the decision points do not have to be analyzed at once. They can be examined one at a time. Consider, for example, the decision to detain arrestees in jail during the pretrial period. A relatively straightforward analysis can empirically illustrate the number and characteristics of arrestees who are booked into jail as opposed to those who are released with a summons or promise to appear (citation) in lieu of jail. The result of the analysis can be a simple table listing arrest offenses and the number and percentage of arrestees for each offense who were booked or cited, by arresting agency.

Incomplete Analysis

The fourth common problem is that even when needed information is available, there is often a lack of skilled personnel and/or time to analyze it. The remedy here is to hire and train justice system planner/analysts and to strengthen planning mechanisms at the agency, city/county, and comprehensive planning levels.

Exhibit 7. The Seven Key Justice System Decision Points

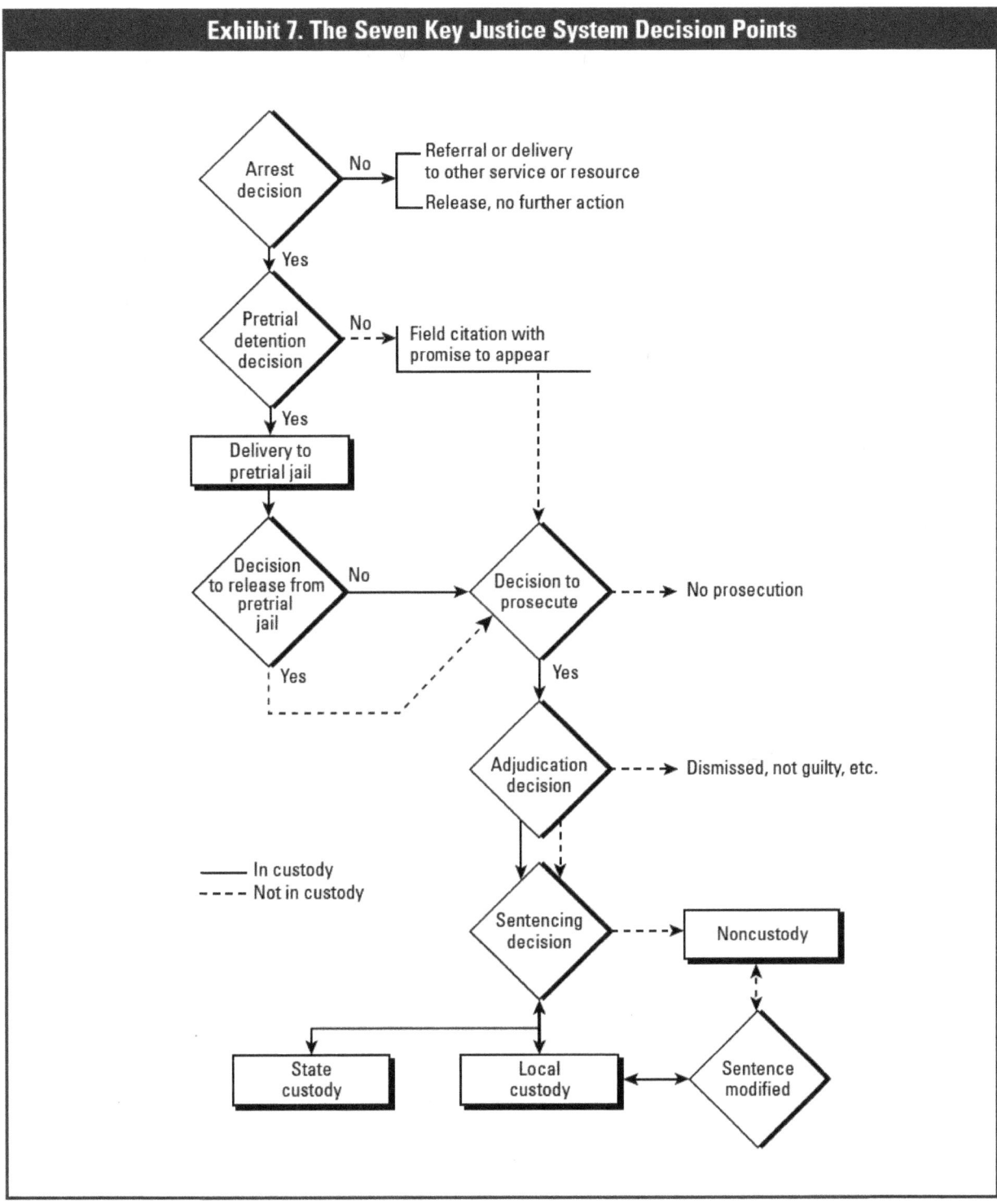

Coordinating Mechanisms— A Developmental View

"Criminal justice coordinating committee" is an inclusive term applied to informal and formal committees that provide a forum within which a large number of key justice system agency officials and other officials of general government may discuss justice system issues. The form and structure of these groups vary.

One way to understand the differences among justice system coordinating groups is to think about a process in which a jurisdiction might move through developmental stages, as if it were on an evolutionary journey. The coordinating mechanisms at each stage of this evolution represent incremental improvements. Each stage is valuable, serves a useful purpose, and then gives way to an increasingly more formalized and more comprehensive organization. This is the general trajectory, but there will be many exceptions.

Informal Coordination

In the most basic circumstances, meetings among officials are likely to be informal. In these jurisdictions, justice system coordination depends almost entirely on well-established, informal communication and person-to-person relationships. This can work well in less populous jurisdictions. If the justice system operating within the jurisdiction is small enough and manageable enough, the leadership can accurately understand the "whole." At a certain size, however, this informal arrangement proves to be inadequate. As a jurisdiction's criminal justice system becomes larger and more complex, more standardized coordination mechanisms are necessary to avoid problems with communication, cooperation, and coordination.

The Justice Forum

The next developmental step involves gathering a group of justice officials to establish a forum for information sharing. These informal meetings may or may not be regularly scheduled. The membership is not comprehensive; that is, it rarely includes city, county, and state levels of government and representatives from all three branches of government.

Adjudication Partnerships

Adjudication partnerships, another important step toward comprehensiveness, are defined as follows:

An adjudication partnership is a formal or informal collaborative effort in which representatives of key justice system agencies join together in multiagency task forces, steering committees, or planning groups to:

1. Identify and discuss a problem.

2. Develop goals and strategies for addressing the problem.

3. Oversee the implementation of a plan to manage or solve the problem.

Ideally, the membership of an adjudication partnership will include the three primary players in any adjudication process: the prosecution, the defense, and the court.

The underlying concept of the adjudication partnership is not new. It serves as an umbrella concept under which many interagency efforts can be classified.[10]

Adjudication partnerships are being encouraged through a cooperative effort of the American Prosecutor's Research Institute, the National Center for State Courts, and the National Legal Aid and Defender's Association. The American Prosecutors Research Institute and the National Center for State Courts have identified 103 adjudication partnerships through a national mail survey.

The Justice Task Force

The single feature that characterizes this developmental stage is that an authorized authority makes appointments to a task force and gives it a "charge," which is often a single, pressing issue. For example, as shown in the sample charge provided in this document (appendix D), a jurisdiction may form a jail task force to deal with jail crowding. Task forces represent a formal acknowledgment that improved planning and coordination must take place. One weakness of this approach is that it may not be comprehensive enough. For example, establishing a jail task force narrowly defines the situation as a "jail problem" or the "sheriff's problem," rather than as a systemwide problem or justice system dysfunction.

Jail crowding is less a problem to solve than it is a systemwide condition that needs to be continuously managed.

—Richard Geaither, National Institute of Corrections, Jails Division

---

In other situations, the formation of a special task force may be more informal. For example, in Dakota County, Minnesota, the local director of community corrections successfully formed an intermediate sanctions task force, melding together a group of justice officials who had never worked well together in the past.

County or City Justice Planning Units

Often justice planning and coordination efforts are confined to the jurisdictional boundaries of a

city or county government. This is a "go it alone" approach, in which a city/county attempts to focus its efforts only on agencies that are part of the city or the county. Often, this approach is control oriented, based on the philosophy that if you are not responsible for it, you cannot control it.

A few months ago, the mayor changed the name of the agency to the Mayor's Office on Criminal Justice. The mayor had recognized for some time that it is not feasible for the mayor to coordinate the justice system in this city because he really controls only one of the many agencies that make up the system—the police department. All of the other parts of the system are administered by other levels of government. This diversity weakens the ability of the mayor or any other public official to effectively coordinate the system.

—Respondent to a request for CJCC information in a major U.S. city

---

Regional Justice Planning Units

The 1968 Omnibus Crime Control and Safe Streets Act created the Law Enforcement Assistance Administration (LEAA) and outlined the means by which state and local units of government would receive federal support for criminal justice planning and action. The LEAA established a grant program to help state and local governments expand their planning capabilities. To receive these funds, a locality or group of localities needed to form a regional planning unit (RPU). Grants management dominated the agendas of most of the RPUs.

By the time the LEAA program was phased out in 1982, the RPUs that existed primarily to garner and administer federal grant funds disappeared. But others evolved to the point where federal initiatives, although still important, no longer served as the primary stimulus. These local units increasingly targeted the bulk of their resources on analysis, coordination, technical assistance, and other planning activities undertaken for the benefit of all local justice agencies within the county or region. Many RPUs reinvented themselves as CJCCs, including the Louisville-Jefferson County (Kentucky) Crime Commission, established more than 30 years ago and probably the oldest continuously operating CJCC in the United States; the Toledo-Lucas County (Ohio) Criminal Justice Coordinating Council; and the Los Angeles Countywide Criminal Justice Coordination Committee.

Corrections Advisory Boards

Many states have passed community corrections acts, encouraging localities to limit commitments to the state prison system (and thus create local corrections options) and to strengthen traditional jail and probation operations. In return for financial aid, the community corrections acts require localities to form a broad-based local corrections advisory board and an annual plan. This provides many communities with motivation, structure, and valuable experience in improving justice system coordination.

While these coordination mechanisms are heavily focused on the corrections subsystem, they often perform many of the more comprehensive functions associated with a CJCC. In fact, in several states—Oregon and Colorado, for example—the corrections advisory boards were a direct stepping stone to the eventual legislative mandate for CJCCs.

Oregon counties with particularly strong local justice coordination groups include Marion, Jackson, Josephine, Benton, and Malheur. Several smaller counties—Wasco, Hood River, Gilliam, and Sherman—have banded together to jointly build and operate a regional correctional facility.

—Representative, Oregon State Community Corrections

Jefferson County, Colorado, is one example. It has a strong local justice coordination group that built on the prior experience of a local community corrections advisory board and other related coordination mechanisms.

An Ideal Criminal Justice Coordinating Committee

The ideal CJCC would have the following characteristics:

- Encompass broad representation, recognized authority, and adequate staff support.

- Include representation of city, county, and state levels of government operating within the geographic boundary of a county or region.

- Include representatives of all functional components of the justice system.

- Involve citizens on the CJCC, committees, or both.

- Be established by an intergovernmental agreement; its role would be spelled out in a written statement of purpose.

- Receive funding, in part, from each member agency to ensure a political and financial stake.

- Enjoy the support and willing participation of all members, who collectively carry great weight and prestige.

- Remain administratively independent so that no one jurisdiction or justice system component would control the organization.

- Ensure that the staff includes a sufficient number of professionals with criminal justice experience, technical skills, and analytical capabilities.

Coordination groups with the characteristics described above are still rare. Many jurisdictions have not yet arrived at the point where they have the analysis and coordination capabilities that are the hallmark of a modern, systems-oriented CJCC. Many also lack comprehensiveness.

> *Seven critical elements were observed in successful adjudication partnership efforts. These critical elements are leadership; broad-based membership; clear, useful, and achievable goals; a team approach; a long-term view; a commitment to using new information and monitoring progress; and criminal justice system and community support. . . . Together, these critical elements provide a solid basis for criminal justice leaders and managers to coordinate and collaborate with other agencies to address significant needs and problems in their jurisdictions.*
>
> —Member, adjudication partnership,
> quoted in Jane Nady Sigmon et al.,
> *Adjudication Partnerships: Critical Components*[11]

Still, in many places, justice planning in any of these forms results in improved communication, cooperation, and coordination; a better understanding of the nature of crime and justice system problems; and greater efficiency and effectiveness in operations. These jurisdictions can advance to the forefront by incorporating the elements identified as characteristic of successful local CJCCs.

Guiding Principles for CJCCs

Research and experience have produced a "collective wisdom" about how to create, staff, evaluate, and rejuvenate CJCCs. General guidelines derived from these principles are discussed in this section. Lessons learned from the Juvenile Detention Alternative Initiative (JDAI) include the following:

The Juvenile Detention Alternative Initiative has shown that detention systems can change when key policy-level system actors come together and do three things: (1) develop consensus (relying heavily on data) about what is wrong with the system; (2) develop a vision of what the new system should look like; and (3) develop and implement a plan of action.

In pursuing these three activities, seven principles emerged from the successes and failures of the JDAI sites:

1. Forming a collaborative group for system reform is extremely hard work and will take longer than you think.

2. For collaboration to work, all the relevant stakeholders must be at the table.

3. In collaboration-driven reforms, the group must develop consensus about what should change and how it should change.

4. There's no real collaboration without negotiation and willingness to compromise.

5. Without strong and able leaders, reform is unlikely.

6. Collaborative leadership must include a jurisdiction's "movers and shakers."

7. Self-assessment and data are essential engines for effective collaboration.[12]

Creating a Criminal Justice Coordinating Committee

Who initiates action, or by whose authority is action initiated? How does a CJCC get started? The answers to these questions vary, depending on the locality and the situation.

If there is concern about jail crowding, then that's where you start. Give them something important to do. Start with an assessment of the current situation. Create a vision of what the system should look like. Engage them in closing the gap between what exists and what is desired.

—Bob Maccarone, former Staff Director, Westchester County (New York) Criminal Justice Advisory Board

---

Consultants who provide onsite technical assistance on behalf of the National Institute of Corrections commonly find that a community asks for technical assistance because there is uncertainty and ambiguity about who can legitimately take action or how to proceed, not because they are unaware that the situation needs attention.

The source of initiative for change can come from unlikely sources. Often, it comes from a problem everyone is concerned about. For example, a crisis can lead to increased collaboration.

Key justice agency leaders and officials of general government must provide leadership. One or more of these men and women must step forward. This leadership is most likely to emerge during times of change or crisis.

In other situations, a CJCC may emerge simply because of the cumulative weight of financial pressure. It may be nothing specific, other than a general sense that justice system expenditures are growing faster than those of general government, or recognition that the growth rate of justice agency workloads is simply not sustainable. CJCCs provide a way for officials who worry about budgets to involve themselves in the process earlier. In these situations, the CJCC may emerge slowly and incrementally.

> *In the early days, when energy is high but skepticism is rampant, it helps to establish a beachhead from which to work by doing something that feels like a group success. Later, when members feel that they belong to a group, more intractable obstacles can be addressed. It is important to begin with a few simple challenges, prove they can be overcome, and then move onto the bigger ones.*
>
> **—Kathleen Feely,** *Collaboration and Leadership in Juvenile Detention Reform*[13]

Holding a daylong workshop, with assistance from a skilled facilitator, in a retreat setting is one good way to initiate a CJCC. These workshops might be repeated, at least annually, as a way to refocus and reenergize the CJCC.

Relationship to State Justice Planning Function

CJCCs are more likely to be created and to succeed in states where state government encourages local criminal justice planning, analysis, and coordination. State governments can play a powerful role by assisting and empowering local jurisdictions. They can help localities define the needs of their communities, support local efforts to develop balanced and systemic solutions, and obtain data to guide decisionmaking.

State agencies also benefit by developing and maintaining relationships with CJCCs. Including representatives of local CJCCs on state criminal justice planning agency boards, committees, and task forces will forge important links to improve state and local justice planning and coordination.

Suggested guidelines for states to promote better state/local justice coordination partnerships include the following:

- Ensure that state officials operating at the local level have been expected to participate and provide information for local planning efforts.

- Provide technical or financial assistance to enhance local efforts in data collection and analysis for policy purposes.

- Provide support and assistance in the development of local coordinating councils and training on policy planning.

- Provide incentives through grant awards for jurisdictions with planning boards and for jurisdictions that see the "big picture" and recognize systemic and fiscal impacts of new projects.

- Recognize there are no "cookie-cutter" approaches; avoid attempting to impose homogeneity in an environment marked by variety.

- Acknowledge that states and localities must try to overcome their negative history and agree to disagree on some issues.[14]

Some states have deliberately fostered the formation of local CJCCs, either as comprehensive criminal justice planning bodies or through community corrections act legislation. Oregon and Colorado are two states that have migrated toward more comprehensive CJCCs. These states built on successful experiences with community corrections acts that required state and local partnerships to improve local corrections operations through better planning, analysis, and coordination. Maryland, Pennsylvania, and Virginia have statewide initiatives that promote collaboration across justice system components and focus on concerns and priorities at the community level.[15]

Geographic Scope

Justice system planning is enhanced when it encompasses as complete a "system" of justice as possible. CJCCs benefit from geographic boundaries that are coterminous within the jurisdictional boundaries of a local justice system. Normally, this means a geographic area with the same boundaries as a county. Municipalities usually invest heavily in police services, and counties are more involved in court and correctional services. Thus, if a CJCC's coverage extends to the county boundaries, it usually deals with a complete, or nearly complete, local justice system. Even in jurisdictions with many state-administered criminal justice activities, a countywide arrangement usually pulls together most locally administered functions.

This principle leads to related notions, for example, that joint city/county CJCCs are generally preferable to either single-city or county-only CJCCs. Geography is less important than the *range* of justice functions falling within the jurisdiction of the CJCC.

A different set of guidelines appears to govern smaller cities and counties without major population centers. Smaller cities and counties can effectively combine their resources to support a comprehensive multicounty CJCC effort that none could provide alone. Small counties can be grouped in different ways. One approach is to encourage them to fall together into natural groups based on local preference or traditional intercounty alliances, such as a council of governments. Another is to organize around existing multicounty judicial districts.

Authorization and Purpose

Many coordinating groups operate informally, for example, at the request of a mayor, judge, or chief administrative officer. The effectiveness of the group, however, will be enhanced by a degree of independence and the legitimacy accorded by formal authorization. A first step in setting up a local coordinating body of the kind envisioned here is to obtain legal authorization for the CJCC to serve as a cross-agency and cross-jurisdictional planning and coordination mechanism. For example, the CJCC might be established by a joint resolution of local governments, a joint

powers agreement, a municipal ordinance, a resolution of the county government, a statute, or an executive order.

A clearly articulated purpose and mission statement should be prepared and formally adopted. Whatever form of enabling mechanism is used, its provisions should describe the CJCC's location within local government and its major purposes, duties, and powers, and outline the mutual responsibilities of the CJCC and the agencies it serves. Such a document will legitimize CJCC staff efforts to obtain line agency cooperation in collecting necessary data and to implement CJCC-sponsored plans and programs.

Structure

Most CJCCs with advanced practices are city/county collaborations. Typically, they are independent from the city and/or county administrative structure. The staff, too, is responsible to the CJCC, although they may be housed in a city or county office building.

All CJCCs have a chairperson and many also have a vice-chair. Normally, these two individuals also serve on a steering committee or executive committee that is usually required because the total CJCC membership is so large. In addition, most CJCCs have both standing and special purpose committees. For example, some have standing committees that mirror the police, courts, and corrections components of the justice system. CJCCs also may form interdisciplinary committees to consider specific problem areas, such as jail crowding or juvenile matters. These may be standing committees or committees formed for a specific duration. CJCCs often establish subcommittees that pull staff from several agencies. For example, some subcommittees include a particularly knowledgeable middle manager and technical experts who are subordinates to CJCC members.

Some CJCCs, such as the Los Angeles Countywide Criminal Justice Coordination Committee, consist solely of justice system officials. Others include citizens.

Bylaws

Bylaws should be developed to govern the day-to-day business of the CJCC and to delineate the specific powers and duties of the CJCC, its members, and its staff. The development of bylaws formalizes the process of creating a skeleton of an agreement that can serve as the basis for a CJCC (see appendix E for sample bylaws for a CJCC).

Representation and Membership

The CJCC should be governed by a membership that is broadly representative of both local elected officials of general government and elected and appointed criminal justice agency administrators from within the county's geographic boundaries. It might also include personnel of certain nonjustice agencies and private citizens. Because it deals with a number of agencies and more than one unit of government, the CJCC should be an independent body. Independence and broad representation help provide the systemwide perspective necessary for comprehensiveness, and policy direction by local government and justice officials ensures greater responsiveness to local needs.

The Tarrant County Criminal Justice Planning Group (CJPG) is chaired by community volunteers, representative of the Tarrant County community, who serve in a "countywide" capacity. The CJPG has produced a Community Plan for Criminal Justice.

—Les Smith, Manager, Criminal Justice Programs, Tarrant County Administrator's Office, Fort Worth, Texas

The CJCC should include four categories of members: (1) justice officials, (2) officials of general government, (3) officials of related nonjustice agencies, and (4) statesmen. Justice officials form the core of these broad-based CJCCs, but this core should be embedded in a larger, more comprehensive community-based context that goes beyond the interests of the justice constituency.

There is an important distinction between a committee made up of justice officials and a committee that also includes officials of general government (e.g., a county commissioner, city or county manager, or mayor) and of related agencies (e.g., the health department, school, or social services agencies).

Broad-based representation helps to ensure that every agency affected by changes. . . has the opportunity to offer valuable insights regarding the plan for achieving program goals. This strategy also helps to prevent agencies that are not included in the planning process and/or that do not agree with the mission, goals, or strategy from scuttling a program or delaying its implementation.

—Jane Nady Sigmon et al., Adjudication Partnerships: Critical Components[16]

CJCCs also benefit from "statesmen"—one or two community leaders who are not justice system experts and have no special interest in any portion of the justice system. These statesmen can establish a sense of altruism in the CJCC by insisting, "We expect you to get along together. We expect you to solve these problems." They may also ask discerning questions. A broad base of support is important, but citizen members representing special interests should not be added; the CJCC will most likely have too many already.

Board membership should be specified in the bylaws along with the principles governing methods and terms of appointment. Overlapping terms of at least one year are important for continuity in board composition. For example, the bylaws of the Marion County, Oregon, Public Safety Coordinating Council stipulate that, at a minimum, membership must consist of:

• A police chief selected by police chiefs in the county.

• The county district attorney.

- A public defender or defense attorney.

- A county commissioner.

- A health/mental health director.

- City council member or mayor.

- A representative of the Oregon State Police (nonvoting).

- The county sheriff.

- A state court judge.

- A director of community corrections.

- A juvenile department director.

- At least one lay citizen.

- A city manager or another city representative.

- A representative of the Oregon Youth Authority (nonvoting).

Achieving broad participation may result in a large CJCC, so some balance must be worked out. For example, counties with a large number of cities may have too many local police chiefs to include on the CJCC. The solution is to invite the chair of the local association of police chiefs to participate.

Selecting the Chair

Selecting the CJCC chair almost always elicits comments about the requirements of leadership. Staff and members of CJCCs have made many observations about a chair's needed characteristics, including the following:

- We need a leader as opposed to a manager.

- He or she must have the respect of the group.

- Integrity is key.

- When they chair, it's for the good of the group.

- Our chair runs a "tight and fair" meeting.

- Everyone gets their say.

- If you stack the deck, it won't help you any.

Establishing "an air of altruism" promotes the workings of the CJCC. Using the position as chair to achieve a political advantage signals the probable demise of the CJCC.

For years, the informal practice at our CJCC has been to have a nonjustice professional serve as chair of the CJCC. For example, a professor of criminal justice chaired our CJCC.

—Bob Maccarone, Assistant District Attorney and former Staff Director, Westchester County (New York) Criminal Justice Advisory Board

---

According to Jane Nady Sigmon and colleagues:

[T]he leader must possess certain skills and take on specific responsibilities, including:

- Articulating the current problem.

- Setting forth a vision for how the local justice system will tackle the problem.

- Convincing other key people of its value so it becomes a shared vision.

- Building partnerships to achieve the envisioned change.

The leader also must be able to motivate and inspire people to commit their time and effort to the program and participate as equals around a table, despite real or perceived differences between members in power and status.[17]

Leadership will change over time. The CJCC will need to plan for leadership transitions to avoid crises when they occur.

> *Real reform is not possible without taking risks. Collaborative work mitigates that risk. One of the benefits of collaborative change structures is that once the group builds its strength and gets a sense of its power, it realizes that risks can be taken more readily. When the whole group has developed consensus about what should be done, it represents a united front of experts speaking with one voice. This is a formidable voice, one that is difficult to ignore. Collaborative leaders are wise if they are able to gauge when and how to use this voice, this power, and when not to. Leadership must manage this newly found power carefully.*
>
> **—Kathleen Feely, *Collaboration and Leadership in Juvenile Detention Reform*[18]**

Executive Committee and Standing Committees

The purposes and composition of an executive committee and standing committees and task forces must be determined. It is important to recognize that the need for staff support will increase as the CJCC forms committees and task forces. Larger boards almost always need an executive committee.

> *In Marion County, Oregon, the Executive Steering Committee of the Public Safety Coordinating Council meets on the last Tuesday of each month for the primary purpose of developing meeting agendas for the full council. The members include the chair and vice chair of the council and representatives of both a city police department and the Marion County Sheriff's Office.*
>
> **—Bylaws, Marion County Public Safety Coordinating Council[19]**

Voting

The bylaws of most CJCCs address voting, and most refer to a majority rule. In practice, however, many CJCCs do not actually bring issues to a vote; instead, decisions are usually made by consensus. But consensus is not always the rule. For example, when an issue comes up for a vote at the Hennepin County/City of Minneapolis CJCC, it is not adopted unless there is unanimous agreement.

> *The CJCC will not survive long if every issue that comes to the table is controversial and results in bloodshed.*
>
> **—John O'Sullivan, former Staff Director, Hennepin County/City of Minneapolis Criminal Justice Coordinating Committee**

The potential for a vote tends to level the playing field in which separate agencies usually differ in terms of power and authority. Representatives from small jurisdictions have an equal opportunity to express their views, and, if a vote is taken, their vote often carries the same weight as a larger jurisdiction.

Some jurisdictions, concerned about attendance, permit only the official members to vote. This means their subordinates can attend and represent them, but they cannot vote and they do not count toward a quorum.

Setting the Agenda

A clear agenda, delivered well in advance, will help promote attendance. It should include items that are clearly relevant to the participants. Informational matters and operational-level concerns should be kept to a minimum so that policy-level discussion and action can take place. As a general rule, the CJCC does not meddle in the internal affairs of any single justice agency. Agenda items focus on issues that cut across agency interests or operations. Typically, this shifts the emphasis away from looking at individual agencies and refocuses attention on the decision points where they come together to do their work, as was shown in exhibit 7.

> *The presiding judge of the court chairs the cabinet, and there are regularly scheduled meetings. The meetings are structured. Items on the agenda are timed, and agendas are distributed a week in advance.*
>
> **—Mary Ann Treadaway, Staff Member, Sacramento County (California) Criminal Justice Cabinet**

In most CJCCs, the chair develops the agenda in concert with the staff. Members are encouraged to submit agenda items to the staff and/or the chair. They have an *obligation* to do so if an upcoming initiative is likely to affect other parts of the justice system.

Meetings

The CJCC should meet regularly, either monthly or quarterly. A schedule of future meeting dates and times should be agreed upon well in advance of the meetings. The meetings must be well organized and well run.

> *Discussions at meetings should be open, frank, and civil. Exhibiting civility and respect for others is critical in fostering cooperation and helping steering committee members grow in their understanding of the problems and needs of each of the participating agencies.*
>
> **—Jane Nady Sigmon et al., Adjudication Partnerships: Critical Components[20]**

Financing the CJCC

Once the objectives and priorities have been set, planning activities identified, and staff needs outlined, an overall CJCC budget must be estimated and the sources of funds considered. Federal or state funds may be primary sources, particularly in the early stages of CJCC development, but local government revenues are a significant source in many jurisdictions.

Local financial investments help institutionalize the planning process within the general structure of local government, giving it greater stability and orienting it more directly to local issues. Shared local government funding also prevents domination of the CJCC by one jurisdiction or justice system component and provides a sense of commitment from all of the members.

> *Our CJCC is governed by a joint powers agreement containing a formula for funding by the participating jurisdictions. This is a county made up of many cities, none being dominant in size or assessed evaluation.*
>
> **—Cynthia Brandon, Executive Director, San Mateo County (California) Criminal Justice Council**

This suggests that federal and/or state financial assistance be concentrated on encouraging and initiating or enhancing local planning and coordination competencies for more self-sustaining operations. The financial contribution of local governments then should be incrementally increased as local officials become convinced that the CJCC's planning, analysis, and coordination activities serve important local needs.

Staffing the CJCC

The staff support provided to the CJCC will largely depend on the size of the jurisdiction and the resources available, but a CJCC will not work well unless it receives independent, full-time staff support. The Hennepin County/City of Minneapolis CJCC has its own budget and dedicated staff who report directly to county administration. Before the 1977 reorganization of the CJCC, it had no legal status, no budget, and no full-time staff. CJCC accomplishments depended on part-time staff contributed by member agencies and available funding.

> *The cabinet is supported by a full-time senior administrative analyst. Funding for this position is shared by the agencies of the executive committee. In addition, the cabinet is supported by a contracted research consultant. The cabinet staff is responsible for monitoring his work plan and deliverables. The county funds this contract.*
>
> **—Mary Ann Treadaway, Staff Member, Sacramento County (California) Criminal Justice Cabinet**

Planning for staffing needs should be preceded by careful consideration of CJCC objectives. The number of staff members and their qualifications will be determined by the types of planning, analysis, and coordination activities they will undertake. Members of the CJCC should invest some time in preliminary planning to maximize staff effectiveness. This is a "preparing for planning" step, as shown in exhibit 5, the 11-step general planning process model.

> *A wide variety of skills is needed. These are rarely found in a single individual. The traditional system designer-expediter is still needed, but so is the entrepreneurially minded new venture analyst, so is an analytic diagnostician-controller, so is a skilled forecaster-analyst, so is a computer-model builder.*
>
> **—H. Igor Ansoff, quoted in John K. Hudzik and Gary W. Cordner, *Planning in Criminal Justice Organizations and Systems*[21]**

Staff members will need skills in three basic areas. First, they should have analytical skills and experience. They should be able to collect and analyze data and convert the data into useful information. This ability will depend on the second basic skill area: practical experience and an understanding of justice system agencies and processes. The third skill area involves political, managerial, and administrative capacities to get along well with CJCC members and justice agencies.

The CJCC staff should be characterized by credibility, neutrality, and stability. Credibility with justice agencies and local government officials comes with demonstrated competence and neutrality and from the legitimacy associated with formal authorization to serve in an interagency and interjurisdictional role. Neutrality must be conscientiously practiced by the staff director and subordinates but can be promoted by insulating the CJCC staff from local politics (basing staffing on the merit system rather than on political appointments). Stability of the unit, essential to the continuity of long-range planning, is enhanced by protection from political involvement, by strong enabling legislation, and by efforts to institutionalize planning within the local government structure.

> *Flexibility needs to be part of the job description.*
>
> **—Ann Bowland, Toledo-Lucas County (Ohio) Criminal Justice Coordinating Council**

In successful CJCCs, the staff director and the chair of the CJCC have a close, compatible, and effective working relationship. The best of both worlds is to have a talented justice planner as staff director and an effective leader as chair.

Typical Staff Assignments

The work of the CJCC can be illustrated by a quick summary of typical staff assignments. As shown earlier in exhibit 2, staff assignments may include any of the following:

- Developing databases.

- Staffing CJCC subcommittees.

- Conducting legislative analyses.

- Gathering or disseminating public information.

- Coordinating agency efforts.

- Mediating interagency disputes.

- Helping agencies articulate goals and priorities.

- Planning for resource allocation and reviewing agency budgets.

- Preparing grant applications and managing grants.

- Designing, implementing, and evaluating programs.

- Providing technical assistance, training, and information brokerage services.

- Conducting special studies and a wide range of analysis activities.

Evaluating the CJCC

Evaluation of the CJCC can do much to convince taxpayers that justice agencies are doing their job and that justice dollars are well spent. A general evaluation approach is shown in exhibit 8. Polling the CJCC members should be part of any evaluation of the CJCC. Public opinion surveys can also provide measures of public satisfaction with the local justice system.

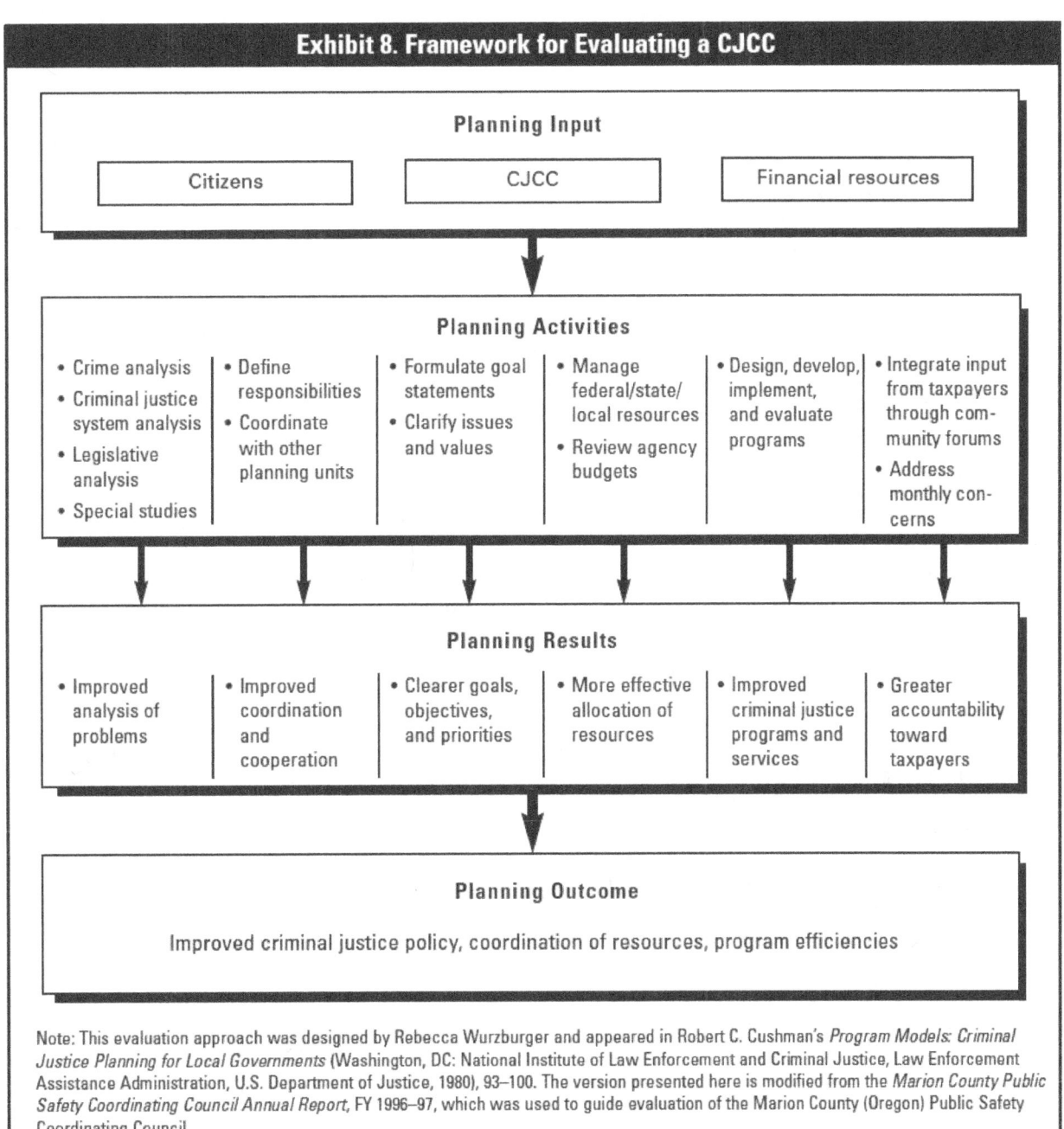

Exhibit 8. Framework for Evaluating a CJCC

Planning Input

| Citizens | CJCC | Financial resources |

Planning Activities

- Crime analysis
- Criminal justice system analysis
- Legislative analysis
- Special studies

- Define responsibilities
- Coordinate with other planning units

- Formulate goal statements
- Clarify issues and values

- Manage federal/state/ local resources
- Review agency budgets

- Design, develop, implement, and evaluate programs

- Integrate input from taxpayers through community forums
- Address monthly concerns

Planning Results

- Improved analysis of problems

- Improved coordination and cooperation

- Clearer goals, objectives, and priorities

- More effective allocation of resources

- Improved criminal justice programs and services

- Greater accountability toward taxpayers

Planning Outcome

Improved criminal justice policy, coordination of resources, program efficiencies

Note: This evaluation approach was designed by Rebecca Wurzburger and appeared in Robert C. Cushman's *Program Models: Criminal Justice Planning for Local Governments* (Washington, DC: National Institute of Law Enforcement and Criminal Justice, Law Enforcement Assistance Administration, U.S. Department of Justice, 1980), 93–100. The version presented here is modified from the *Marion County Public Safety Coordinating Council Annual Report*, FY 1996–97, which was used to guide evaluation of the Marion County (Oregon) Public Safety Coordinating Council.

> *The Palm Beach County (Florida) Criminal Justice Commission currently has a consultant evaluating their work and accomplishments.*
>
> **—Sally Graham, Criminal Justice Policy Coordinator, Sarasota County, Florida**

The Marion County Public Safety Coordinating Council has conducted several surveys to measure public opinion about justice services and priorities. The objectives of the public opinion surveys were to:

- Identify registered voter opinions about the most important issue facing Marion County government, with reference to crime.

- Identify registered voter attitudes toward specific statements about fighting crime and about Marion County government.

- Identify whether registered voters support construction of a juvenile detention facility and a juvenile justice center.

- Identify how registered voters would spend money between adult and juvenile corrections; prevention, intervention, and treatment programs; juvenile delinquency programs; and prevention programs for families with children.

Hiring an outside consultant, or requesting an evaluation from the National Institute of Corrections, may lead to a more formal and more deliberate evaluation of the CJCC.

Rejuvenating the CJCC

CJCCs are fragile: Some atrophy; others pass away entirely. In a survey of 30 CJCCs, respondents were asked to list the factors that significantly contributed to and detracted from the success of their CJCC.[22]

The most important *contributing* factors for success were identified as (1) good relationships with criminal justice agencies and officials of general government; (2) the CJCC's nonpartisan image and multijurisdictional approach; and (3) dedicated staff with technical ability. These assets keep a CJCC healthy; therefore, they should be actively promoted. (Leadership, citizen support, and adequate financial support were mentioned less frequently as contributing factors.)

The factors that most *detracted* from success were (1) financial constraints; (2) staffing reductions; and (3) conflicts between agencies (over "turf"). These danger signs will need attention if a CJCC is to remain healthy.

Rejuvenating a CJCC involves answering three questions:

- What happened to the previous CJCC?

- What has changed?

- Who should revive the CJCC?

What Happened to the Previous CJCC?

Surveying previous members is a good place to begin answering this question. Chances are that the previous CJCC had weak scores on the CJCC self-evaluation questionnaire presented as exhibit 1 of this guide.

> *Ask: "How is the justice system less viable because the CJCC is gone?" It's likely that asking this question will help officials identify many things a CJCC could help them accomplish that they cannot possibly accomplish on their own.*
>
> **—Ann Bowland, Toledo-Lucas County (Ohio) Criminal Justice Coordinating Council**

Interagency conflict can cause the demise of a CJCC. But, after a period, it may be possible to revive the CJCC and start again. Another common problem is that interest wanes when a CJCC drifts from a policy-planning orientation and becomes consumed with operational concerns.

What Has Changed?

CJCCs are rarely static. They change and adapt, or they deteriorate and die. If a CJCC is dependent on an unusually strong and effective leader, it will likely suffer when leadership changes. Elections will remove some members and new ones will replace them, possibly threatening the continuity the CJCC needs to survive. Newly elected and appointed officials may see the CJCC as a vestige of old philosophies and old ways of doing things. A new executive order, a new mission statement, a new challenge, or a reorganization may be needed to help them "own" the process.

> In 1997, the Hennepin County/City of Minneapolis CJCC spent much of the year evaluating its effectiveness and direction. The end result was a reorganization, the adoption of a vision and mission statement, and a formal cooperative agreement between the City of Minneapolis and Hennepin County outlining organizational basics and funding responsibilities. The new organization has fewer members with a slightly stronger suburban emphasis. In addition, a vice-chair position was added along with a provision for the orderly transfer of the chair.
>
> —John O'Sullivan, former Staff Director, Hennepin County/City of Minneapolis Criminal Justice Coordinating Committee

Opportunities to reinvigorate a CJCC may come from new or pending legislation that is expected to affect justice system workloads. Examples include increased criminal penalties for drinking/driving offenses, a three-strikes law, and changes in state/local responsibilities for supervising offenders in custody or in the community. Each of these may represent an opportunity to call the local justice leadership together to conduct problem-oriented planning.

Who Should Revive the CJCC?

Reviving the CJCC is a shared responsibility, but someone must take the lead. Often, two or more officials can agree to sponsor revival of the CJCC.

An early meeting in a retreat or workshop setting, with a trained facilitator, can help a CJCC get off to a healthy, vigorous new start. Where possible, efforts to rejuvenate a CJCC should start small and build competence gradually. Organizers should avoid spending too much time and energy bringing one or two naysayers into the fold. Instead, they might attempt to build a critical mass of the key players and work "downhill," beginning with tasks in which opportunities for success are the greatest. They should build upon small gains.

Visits to other CJCCs can also help officials see new possibilities. Even a brief telephone conversation with a counterpart in another jurisdiction can help a local official think more optimistically about the potential of a CJCC.

The skills of the CJCC members and staff will develop incrementally as they gain experience and foster the working relationships with agency and government officials necessary for comprehensive local justice planning. As these relationships develop, the CJCC should focus on strengthening the decisionmaking capacities of the cities, counties, and justice agencies in its jurisdiction, helping them to improve the way they provide the services and programs for which they are responsible.

> Any change in one part of the justice system has a ripple effect. Some justice agency executives don't appreciate the systemwide impact of the decisions they make.
>
> —Tom Giacinti, Jefferson County (Colorado) Criminal Justice Strategic Planning Committee

Demonstrating the Benefits

CJCCs need to continuously demonstrate the benefits of their collaborative efforts to member agencies and the community at large. They need to look for opportunities to celebrate and reinforce success. Most CJCCs prepare a list of major accomplishments at least annually. They celebrate success as they achieve key milestones and objectives. For example, the Jail Utilization Systems Team (JUST) Project of Monroe County

(Rochester, New York) released the following public statement:

> In 1992, the Monroe County (Rochester, New York) Executive required all county departments to incorporate total quality management (TQM) and work together to address county problems. Local justice system leaders joined together and developed a multi-part strategy to reduce jail crowding. They developed a continuum of graduated restrictions for out-of-custody pretrial defendants, added graduated sanctioning options for convicted misdemeanants, expedited case processing for prison/jail bound offenders, and strengthened their case processing information system. These actions reduced the average length of jail stay. As a consequence, the daily jail population was reduced by 209 beds, even though jail admissions increased from 13,587 in 1994 to 15,842 for 1997 (20 percent).[23]

Some CJCCs (e.g., the Palm Beach County, Florida, Criminal Justice Commission) have a public relations subcommittee charged with interpreting the results of the CJCC to the public, to other justice agencies, to government officials, and to the media. Effectively communicating each CJCC's success will build support for planning and coordination and ultimately improve local criminal justice programs and services nationwide.

In the world of limited resources and increased demands for system accountability, criminal justice coordinating committees provide forums for the key players within the justice system to work together, leaving their traditionally adversarial relationship behind in the courtroom. By working together toward the larger goal of improving service for the public, it is likely that criminal justice system leaders will also improve the functioning of their individual agencies.

—Mark Cunniff, Executive Director, National Association of Criminal Justice Planners

---

Notes

1. This saying by Casey Stengel has become such a common part of the American lexicon that the original source of the quotation is difficult to establish. Some of the quotations in this guide without full citations are from the author's personal knowledge; others are from communication with the speaker.

2. Lewis Carroll, *Alice's Adventures in Wonderland*, New York: Harcourt Brace, 1999.

3. Christina Morehead, *A Criminal Justice Planning Model for King County*, Seattle, WA: King County Regional Law, Safety and Justice Committee, 1991, p. 24; based on a survey of 30 CJCCs.

4. Ibid., p. 1.

5. Kathleen Feely, *Collaboration and Leadership in Juvenile Detention Reform*, The Pathways to Juvenile Detention Reform Series (a project of the Annie E. Casey Foundation), 1999, p. 12.

6. As quoted in Robert C. Cushman, *Program Models: Criminal Justice Planning for Local Governments*, Washington, DC: U.S. Department of Justice, National Institute of Law Enforcement and Criminal Justice, Law Enforcement Assistance Administration, 1980, p. 9.

7. Jane Nady Sigmon, Ph.D.; John Goerdt, J.D.; Scott Wallace, J.D.; Heike Gramckow, Ph.D., J.D.; Kathy Free; and M. Elaine Nugent et al., *Adjudication Partnerships: Critical Components*, American Prosecutor's Research Institute (Draft) 1999, p. 4.

8. Cushman, *Program Models*, (see note 6) p. 29.

9. Kim Allen, Executive Director, Kentucky Criminal Justice Council, speaking at the annual membership meeting of the National Criminal Justice Association, July 1999, as quoted in *News Update*, the newsletter of the National Association of Criminal Justice Planners, August 1999.

10. Sigmon et al., *Adjudication Partnerships: Critical Components*, (see note 7) p. 1.

11. Ibid., p. 2.

12. Feely, *Collaboration and Leadership in Juvenile Detention Reform*, (see note 5) p. 14.

13. Ibid., p. 32.

14. Kim Allen, Former Executive Director, Kentucky Criminal Justice Council, speaking at the annual membership meeting of the National Criminal Justice Association, July 1999 (see note 9).

15. See "Community-Based Planning: Promoting A Neighborhood Response to Crime" in *Policy and Practice* (Spring 1998), a quarterly publication of the National Criminal Justice Association, 444 N. Capitol St. NW, Suite 618, Washington, DC 20001.

16. Sigmon et al., *Adjudication Partnerships: Critical Components*, (see note 7) p. 3.

17. Ibid., p. 2.

18. Feely, *Collaboration and Leadership in Juvenile Detention Reform*, (see note 5) p. 38.

19. Bylaws of the Marion County Public Safety Coordinating Council, Salem, Oregon, 1999.

20. Sigmon et al., *Adjudication Partnerships: Critical Components*, (see note 7) p. 4.

21. As quoted in John K. Hudzik and Gary W. Cordner, *Planning in Criminal Justice Organizations and Systems*, New York: Macmillan Publishing Co., 1983, p. 134.

22. Morehead, *A Criminal Justice Planning Model*, (see note 3) pp. 111-112.

23. Jail Utilization Systems Team (JUST) Project, Monroe County, Rochester, New York, 1993.

Checklist for Forming a CJCC

☐ Determine the need for and interest in forming (reforming/rejuvenating) a CJCC.

☐ Locate state legislation that mandates or facilitates formation of a CJCC.

☐ Contact a number of potential "core" members. Share this guide with them. Determine whether they will support the formation of a CJCC.

☐ Determine whether an existing group can form the basis for a CJCC or whether a new group must be formed.

☐ Decide on the geographic scope of the CJCC—countywide or other.

☐ Decide who must authorize the CJCC.

☐ Draft a proposed statement of purpose for the CJCC.

☐ Draft an authorization document or charge.

☐ Determine the structure and administrative location.

☐ Draft bylaws for consideration by the CJCC and/or authorizing groups.

☐ Determine representation and membership.

☐ Select the chair.

☐ Determine executive committee and standing committees or task forces.

☐ Decide who votes, when, and how.

☐ Develop guidelines for establishing meeting agendas.

☐ Determine whether a workshop in a retreat setting with a trained facilitator is needed.

☐ Determine financing for the CJCC.

☐ Identify the number and type of staff that will be needed; hire and train staff.

☐ Develop a method for evaluating the CJCC and for reinvigorating it if it begins to go into decline.

☐ Plan ways to celebrate success and demonstrate the benefits of the CJCC.

Jurisdictions Mentioned in This Guide

(Listed alphabetically by county name; county populations are provided in parentheses.)

Benton County, Oregon (78,153)
Benton County Community Corrections
180 NW Fifth Street
Corvallis, OR 97330–4791
Phone: 541–766–6704; fax: 541–766–6758

Dakota County, Minnesota (355,904)
c/o Community Corrections
Dakota County Government Center
1560 Highway 55
Hastings, MN 55033
Phone: 651–438–8288; fax: 651–438–8340

Gilliam County, Oregon (1,915)
Tri-County (Gilliam/Sherman/Wheeler)
 Community Corrections
P.O. Box 685
Condon, OR 97823
Phone: 541–384–2852; fax: 541–384–2853

Hennepin County, Minnesota (1,116,200)
Hennepin County/City of Minneapolis
Criminal Justice Coordinating Committee
Hennepin County Government Center
Suite A–2308
Minneapolis, MN 55487–0238
Phone: 612–348–5032; fax: 612–348–7423

Hood River County, Oregon (20,411)
Hood River County Community Corrections
P.O. Box 301
489 N. Eighth Street
Hood River, OR 97031–0011
Phone: 541–387–6862; fax: 541–386–7822

Jackson County, Oregon (181,269)
Jackson County Community Justice
P.O. Box 1584
123 W. 10th Street
Medford, OR 97501–0450
Phone: 541–774–4900; fax: 541–770–9484

Jefferson County, Colorado (527,056)
Jefferson County Criminal Justice
 Strategic Planning Committee
700 Jefferson County Parkway, #220
Golden, CO 80401
Phone: 303–271–5063; fax: 303–271–4849

Jefferson County, Kentucky (693,604)
Louisville-Jefferson County Crime Commission
231 S. Fifth Street, Suite 300
Louisville, KY 40202
Phone: 502–574–5088; fax: 502–574–5299

Josephine County, Oregon (75,726)
Josephine County Community Corrections
237 SE J Street
Grants Pass, OR 97526
Phone: 541–474–5165; fax: 541–474–5171

Los Angeles County, California (9,519,338)
Countywide Criminal Justice Coordination
 Committee
500 W. Temple Street
520 Hall of Administration
Los Angeles, CA 90012
Phone: 213–974–8398; fax: 213–613–2711

Lucas County, Ohio (455,054)
Toledo-Lucas County Criminal Justice
  Coordinating Council
301 Collingwood Boulevard
Toledo, OH 43602
Phone: 419–244–5819; fax: 419–244–5244

Malheur County, Oregon (31,615)
Malheur County Community Corrections
1682 SW Fourth Street
Ontario, OR 97914
Phone: 541–881–2402; fax: 541–889–8311

Marion County, Oregon (284,834)
Marion County Public Safety Coordinating
  Council
c/o Marion County Board of Commissioners
P.O. Box 14500
Salem, OR 97309
Phone: 503–588–5212; fax: 503–588–5237

Monroe County, New York (735,343)
Monroe County Department of Public Safety
33 N. Fitzhugh Street
Rochester, NY 14614
Phone: 716–428–4989; fax: 716–428–9023

Multnomah County, Oregon (660,486)
Multnomah County Public Safety Coordinating
  Council
421 SW Sixth Avenue, Suite 1075
Portland, OR 97204–1620
Phone: 503–988–5522; fax: 503–306–5538

Napa County, California (124,279)
Napa County Office of Criminal Justice
  Planning
c/o County Administrator
1195 Third Street, Room 310
Napa, CA 94559
Phone: 707–253–4421; fax: 707–253–4176

Orleans Parish, Louisiana (484,674)
Mayor's Criminal Justice Council
c/o Office of the Mayor
Office of Criminal Justice Coordination
Room 8E15, City Hall
New Orleans, LA 70112–2114
Phone 504–565–7100; fax: 504–565–7748

Palm Beach County, Florida (1,131,184)
Palm Beach County Criminal Justice Commission
301 N. Olive Avenue, Suite 1001
West Palm Beach, FL 33401
Phone 561–355–4943; fax: 561–355–4941

Sacramento County, California (1,223,499)
Criminal Justice Cabinet
700 H Street, Room 7650
Sacramento, CA 95814–1280
Phone: 916–874–5833; fax: 916–874–5885

San Mateo County, California (707,161)
San Mateo County Criminal Justice Council
610 Elm Street, #200
San Carlos, CA 94070
Phone: 650–802–4326; fax: 650–591–1772

Sarasota County, Florida (325,957)
Sarasota County Public Safety Coordinating
  Council
1660 Ringling Boulevard, Second Floor
Sarasota, FL 34236
Phone: 941–951–5249; fax: 941–954–4875

Tarrant County, Texas (1,446,219)
Tarrant County Criminal Justice Planning Group
100 E. Weatherford Street
Fort Worth, TX 76196
Phone 817–884–1734; fax: 817–884–1702

Wasco County, Oregon (23,791)
Wasco County Community Corrections
502 Washington Street, Suite 207
The Dalles, OR 97058–2242
Phone: 541–296–9333; fax: 541–296–1739

Westchester County, New York (923,459)
Westchester County Criminal Justice Advisory
  Board
c/o Department of Probation
112 E. Post Road, Third Floor
White Plains, NY 10601
Phone: 914–995–3569; fax: 914–995–6261

Other CJCC Resources

Free Technical Assistance and Training

The following organizations currently provide free onsite technical assistance.

National Institute of Corrections

Provides federally funded, quick turnaround, short-term onsite technical assistance to state and local governments. Also provides federally funded training at the NIC Academy in Longmont, Colorado, and elsewhere, and information services via the NIC Information Center.

For information on services related to jail issues, contact—
NIC Jails Division
1960 Industrial Circle
Longmont, CO 80501
Phone: 800–995–6429; fax: 303–682–0469

For information on services related to probation, parole, and community-based corrections, contact—
NIC Community Corrections Division
320 First Street NW
Washington, DC 20534
Phone: 800–995–6423; fax: 202–307–3361
Web address: *www.nicic.org/about/divisions/comm_corr.htm*

Services: Available services are described in the annual service plan: *Technical Assistance, Information and Training for Corrections Services Plan.* This 37-page document and a separate training calendar can be downloaded in PDF format at *www.nicic.org/pubs/admin.htm.* A printed copy can be obtained from any NIC office. The service plan includes instructions for requesting technical assistance and training.

American Bar Association

American Bar Association/Bar Information Program
ABA Standing Committee on Legal Aid and Criminal Defendants
541 N. Fairbanks Court
Chicago, IL 60611
Phone: 312–988–5765; fax: 312–988–5483
e-mail: *deorass@staff.abanet.org*
Contact: Shubi Deoras

Services: Provides technical assistance and training to state and local governments interested in improving defense services.

American University

American University Criminal Courts Technical Assistance Project
American University Justice Programs Office
American University Brandywine 100
4400 Massachusetts Avenue NW
Washington, DC 20016–8159
Phone: 202–885–2875; fax: 202–885–2885
e-mail: *justice@american.edu*
Web address: *www.american.edu/justice*
Contact: Joe Trotter

Services: American University, in partnership with the National Legal Aid and Defender Association, the Pretrial Services Resource Center, and the Justice Management Institute, provides federally funded technical assistance to serve criminal courts and related adjudication system agencies.

Additional Sources of Technical Assistance

Community Research Associates
309 W. Clark Street
Champaign, IL 61820
Phone: 217–398–3120; fax: 217–398–3132
e-mail: *cra@community-research.com*
Web address: *www.community-research.com*

Services: Provides federally funded onsite technical assistance and training as a service of the U.S. Department of Justice, Bureau of Justice Assistance (BJA), State and Local Training and Technical Assistance Program. Requests must be made through state criminal justice planning agencies to BJA.

Pretrial Services Resource Center
1010 Vermont Avenue NW, Suite 300
Washington, DC 20005
Phone: 202–638–3080; fax: 202–347–0493
e-mail: *psrc@pretrial.org*

Services: Provides assistance concerning establishing and/or strengthening pretrial services programs. Also addresses jail crowding. Reference materials available at no cost. Contractual onsite work available.

Sources of Current Information

The following national organizations provide current information about sources of technical assistance helpful to CJCCs. Most also offer technical assistance, training, and publications. Counterparts may be found at the state level.

General Government

International City/County Management Association
777 North Capitol Street NE, Suite 500
Washington, DC 20002
Phone: 202–289–4262; fax: 202–962–3500
Web address: *www.icma.org*

National Association of Counties
440 First Street NW, 8th Floor
Washington, DC 20001
Phone: 202–393–6226; fax: 202–393–2630
Web address: *www.naco.org*

National League of Cities
1301 Pennsylvania Avenue NW
Washington, DC 20004
Phone: 202–626–3000; fax: 202–626–3043
Web address: *www.nlc.org*

Law Enforcement, Courts and Corrections

National sources that offer technical assistance, training, and publications are listed below. Additional states offer counterparts.

American Bar Association
Criminal Justice Section
740 15th Street NW
Washington, DC 20005
e-mail: *fortinbs@staff.abanet.org*
Web address: *www.abanet.org*

For criminal justice section, see:
www.abanet.org/crimjust/home.html.

For Juvenile Justice Center, see:
www.abanet.org/crimjust/juvjus/home.html.

American Correctional Association
4380 Forbes Boulevard
Lanham, MD 20706–4322
Phone: 800–222–5646
Web address: *corrections.com/aca*

American Jail Association
2053 Day Road, Suite 100
Hagerstown, MD 21740
Phone: 301–790–3930; fax: 301–790–2941
e-mail: *jails@worldnet.att.net*
Web address: *www.corrections.com/aja*

American Probation and Parole Association
c/o the Council of State Governments
P.O. Box 11910
Lexington, KY 40578–1910
Phone: 859–244–8203; fax: 859–244–8001
e-mail: *appa@csg.org*
Web address: *www.appa-net.org*

International Association of Chiefs of Police
515 N. Washington Street
Alexandria, VA 22314–2357
Phone: 703–836–6767; fax: 703–836–4543
Web address: *www.theiacp.org*

International Community Corrections Association
P.O. Box 1987
La Crosse, WI 54602–1987
Phone: 608–785–0200; fax: 608–784–5335
e-mail: *icca@execpc.com*
Web address: *www.iccaweb.org*

National Association of Criminal Justice Planners
P.O. Box 11127
Washington, DC 20008
Phone: 202–347–0501
e-mail: *nacjp76@aol.com*

National Center for State Courts
300 Newport Avenue
Williamsburg, VA 23185
Phone: 757–253–2000; fax: 757–220–0449
Web address: *www.ncsc.online.org*

National District Attorneys Association
90 Canal Center Plaza
Alexandria, VA 22314
Phone: 703–549–9222; fax: 703–836–3195
Web address: *www.ndaa.org*

National Legal Aid and Defender Association
1625 K Street NW, Suite 800
Washington, DC 20006–1604
Phone 202–452–0620; fax: 202–872–1031
e-mail: *info@nlada.org*
Web address: *www.nlada.org*

National Sheriffs' Association
1450 Duke Street
Alexandria, VA 22314–3490
Phone: 703–836–7827
Web address: *www.sheriffs.org*

For jail operations information, see:
www.sheriffs.org/jail_op.htm.

Police Executive Research Forum
1120 Connecticut Avenue NW, Suite 930
Washington DC 20036
Phone: 202–466–7820; fax: 202–466–7826
Web address: *www.policeforum.org*

Sources of Free Publications

Corrections Connection Network
159 Burgin Parkway
Quincy, MA 02169
Phone: 617–471–4445; fax: 617–770–3339
Web address: *www.corrections.com*

National Criminal Justice Reference Service
Phone: 800–851–3420
e-mail: *askncjrs@ncjrs.org*
Web address: *www.ncjrs.org*

Services: Extensive information on criminal and juvenile justice. This collection of clearinghouses supports all bureaus of the U.S. Department of Justice, including the Office of Justice Programs, the National Institute of Justice, Office of Juvenile Justice and Delinquency Prevention, Bureau of Justice Statistics, Bureau of Justice Assistance, Office for Victims of Crime, and Office of National Drug Control Policy.

National Institute of Corrections Information Center
1860 Industrial Circle, Suite A
Longmont, CO 80501
Phone: 800–877–1461
e-mail: *asknicic@nicic.org*

Services: Publications; information brokerage; information search. Prisons, jails, probation, parole, community-based corrections.

Sample Charge: Charge to the Denver Justice System Task Force

The Need

The administration and the city council have determined that the City of Denver needs to develop a more coordinated, policy-driven approach to alleviate crowding in our jails.

Jail crowding is a complex and pressing problem. It needs high-level coordinated leadership and attention.

If we are to understand the causes of jail crowding and develop a consensus for appropriate and cost-effective solutions, we need to learn more about the interaction between the jails and the justice system, particularly between the jails and the justice agencies that use the jail resource.

We also need to create new policy-oriented mechanisms that will position the justice leadership, officials of general government, and the public to work together more effectively so that we can move toward consensus concerning jail space and related issues.

This action is being taken following consideration of a recommendation by consultants provided to the Denver City Council by the National Institute of Corrections (NIC) to "create an intergovernmental, interagency mechanism which will effectively bring together the Administration, the City Council, and the justice agency leadership" (see September 1997 NIC Report).

Creating the Denver Justice System Task Force

The mayor and president of the city council hereby establish the Denver Justice System Task Force. The members of this group are as follows:

- Mayor or designee.

- President of the city council or designee.

- Chair of the Public Safety Committee.

- Manager of safety.

- Police chief.

- Undersheriff.

- Presiding judge, county court.

- City attorney.

- Chief judge, Second Judicial District.

- District attorney.

- Metro Chamber of Commerce designee.

- Interneighborhood cooperation president.

The Denver Justice System Task Force's charge is to:

- Review and act upon the reports and recommendations of consultants provided by NIC, including the September 1997 and October 1997 NIC Reports, which include a blueprint for data collection and analysis.

- Direct and coordinate city and consultant resources to produce a clear and complete understanding of how jail space is currently being used. The task force is expected to oversee an empirically based examination of jail bed utilization.

- Thereafter, and based upon this empirical information, the task force is expected to lead policy development to guide current and future utilization of jail bed space and, where appropriate, the initiation and utilization of other correctional sanctions and options.

Priorities

The task force will focus priority attention on four areas:

- The task force is expected to develop a thorough understanding of who is arrested and to determine the number and characteristics of arrested persons who are (a) detained in a pretrial facility; or (b) cited with a promise to appear in court.

- The task force is expected to develop a robust understanding of (a) persons admitted to the jails; (b) the characteristics of people released from the jails and their lengths of jail stay; and (c) a picture of how bed space is being utilized (jail population snap shot).

- The task force is expected to develop an understanding of how cases are processed from arrest to final disposition, particularly of persons who are spending time in the jail system.

- The task force is expected to develop recommendations about how Denver can better manage its criminal justice population, including issues related to optimal jail space for consideration by policymakers, the public, and criminal justice agencies and stakeholders.

Schedule and Reporting

The task force will develop a detailed work plan and proposed schedule of milestones. Task force members are expected to attend monthly meetings for 3 hours and to contribute agency resources to necessary data collection and policy analysis. The task force is expected to make periodic reports to the mayor, city council, justice agency leadership, and the public.

Sample Bylaws: County of Sacramento Criminal Justice Cabinet, May 1999

Article I: Name

The name of this Cabinet is the Sacramento County Criminal Justice Cabinet, and it will be referred to as the Cabinet in the following bylaws.

Article II: Authority

The Sacramento County Board of Supervisors and the Sacramento City Council established the Cabinet in March 1992.

Article III: Purpose

Section A: Principal Mission

The principal mission of the Cabinet is to study the Sacramento County juvenile and criminal justice system, identify deficiencies, and formulate policy, plans and programs for change when opportunities present themselves. In addition, its mission is to communicate and present planning, financial, operational, managerial, and programmatic recommendations to the agencies represented on the Cabinet.

The Cabinet is committed to providing the coordinated leadership necessary to establish cohesive public policies which are based on research, evaluation and monitoring of policy decisions and program implementations. The Cabinet is committed to innovative corrections programs for adult and juvenile offenders. Through a coordinated planning effort the Cabinet reviews, evaluates and makes policy recommendations on vital criminal justice system issues.

Section B: Guiding Principle

The Cabinet is committed to serve as the planning body for the Criminal and Juvenile Justice System in Sacramento County.

Section C: Recommendations to Board of Supervisors

The Cabinet can make recommendations to public policy boards regarding juvenile and criminal justice system issues.

Article IV: Members

Section A: Membership by Position

There are sixteen voting members of the Cabinet who are members due to the position they hold. These sixteen members serve on the Cabinet for as long as they occupy the position:

- Presiding Judge, Superior Court of California, County of Sacramento

- Presiding Judge, Juvenile Court, Superior Court of California, County of Sacramento

- Sheriff

- District Attorney

- Public Defender

- Chief Probation Officer

- Mayor, City of Sacramento

- Mayor, City of Citrus Heights

- Chief of Police, City of Sacramento

- County Executive

- Sacramento City Manager

- Administrator, Public Protection and Human Assistance Agency

- Director, Department of Health and Human Services

- Director, Department of Human Assistance

- Director, Department of Medical Systems

- County Superintendent of Schools

Section B: Representative Members

There are three voting members of the Cabinet who serve as representatives from the respective governing bodies on which they serve or of which they are a member. The governing body which they represent determines who will serve on the Cabinet and the length of time.

- Member, Board of Supervisors

- Representative from Cities of Folsom, Isleton, Galt

- Judge, Superior Court of California, County of Sacramento

Section C: Ex Officio Members

Members of the Sacramento legislative delegation are non-voting members of the Cabinet.

Article V: Meetings

Section A: Regular Meetings

The Cabinet meets on the second Thursday of July, September, November, January, March and May beginning at 8:00 a.m.

Section B: Designees

Cabinet members may designate one chief staff person to represent them and vote at Cabinet meetings. Any member wishing to appoint a designee is to identify the designee in written correspondence addressed to the Chair of the Cabinet. Designees can be changed only by notifying the Chair in writing.

Section C: Alternate

The Sacramento County Board of Supervisors names a representative and alternate to serve as Cabinet members. The representative may appoint a designee as described in Article V, Section B, to represent the Board of Supervisors when neither the representative nor alternate is available to attend.

Section D: Quorum

A quorum is no less than a simple majority of the total membership. Designees cannot be counted when determining a quorum. Action may be taken by a majority of those present voting and by not less than a majority of the quorum.

Section E: Convening Special Meetings

The Chair of the Cabinet may convene a special meeting. Written notice must be served at least 48 hours in advance. Only items included in the written notice may be discussed or considered.

Section F: Staff Support

Staff support is provided by the Public Protection and Human Assistance Agency to a maximum of 1.5 positions. Costs for such support are shared equally by the members of the Executive Committee.

Article VI: Chair

The Chair of the Cabinet is the Presiding Judge, Superior Court of California, County of Sacramento. In instances when the Chair cannot attend a meeting, one of the other two judicial officers serving on the Cabinet will preside over the meeting as designated by the Presiding Judge.

Article VII: Voting

Each Cabinet member has one vote. Designees may vote on behalf of a member if they have been identified by the member in written correspondence addressed to the Chair.

Article VIII: Committees

Section A: Purpose

To expedite and facilitate the business of the Cabinet and the orderly and efficient consideration of matters coming before it, the following standing committees are established.

Section B: Executive Committee

The Executive Committee is to provide leadership in the planning and implementation of the Cabinet goals by:

- Designating existing structures or creating new structures for the achievement of the Cabinet goals.

- Reviewing implementation plans, timetables and costs and reporting with recommendations on such matters to the Cabinet.

- Reviewing requests made for resources, developing alternatives when appropriate, and making recommendations to the Cabinet for responding to such requests.

- Reviewing and making recommendations regarding other matters delegated to it by the Cabinet.

- Planning the agenda of the Cabinet meetings.

Membership

- Presiding Judge, Superior Court of California, County of Sacramento (Chair)

- Presiding Judge, Juvenile Court, Superior Court of California, County of Sacramento

- Judge, Superior Court of California, County of Sacramento

- Sheriff

- District Attorney

- Public Defender

- Chief Probation Officer

- County Executive

- Chief of Police, City of Sacramento

- Director, Department of Health and Human Services

Meetings

The Executive Committee meets on the second Thursday of August, October, December, February, April and June beginning at 8:00 a.m. Article V, Sections B and C, regarding designees and quorum apply to the Executive Committee meetings.

Section C: Adult Facility Planning and Operations Committee

Section D: Juvenile Institutions, Programs and Court Committee

Section E: Intermediate Punishments Committee

Section F: Streamlining Criminal Prosecution and Court Operations Committee

Section G: Information Exchange Committee (automation)

(Note: The text details the mission and committee memberships of Sections C through G. These are lengthy and, therefore, are not included here.)

Article IX: Parliamentary Authority

Robert's Rules of Order, revised, governs all Cabinet meetings except in instances of conflict between the rules of order and the bylaws of the Cabinet or provision of law.

Article X: Amendment of Bylaws

Proposed amendments to the bylaws are to be included on the agenda of a regularly scheduled Executive Committee meeting. If approved by the Executive Committee, the proposal will be forwarded to the Cabinet at a regularly scheduled meeting for approval. Any action in response to the proposed change in the bylaws taken by the Cabinet becomes effective immediately.